MW00768282

Squires To Knights
Mentoring Our Teenage Boys

Jeff Purkiss

Table of Contents

Forward

The roles and responsibilities designed by God for men have been twisted and distorted beyond recognition. Men do not know how to be men. And our families, communities, churches and nation are paying the price. We must find ways to pass Christ-centered manhood on to our boys.

Philip Lancaster sums it up well: "Our national crisis is a consequence of the crisis of the home, and the crisis of the home is a crisis of male leadership."[1]

Rather than disciples and servants of God, strong spiritual leaders, loving husbands and involved fathers, dedicated providers and courageous protectors – too many men are becoming (brace yourself guys) busy and work-a-holic, unaffectionate and uninvolved, self-oriented and sports-crazed, macho or wimpy, absent and/or abusive, all too often cheating *men*. Our culture simply no longer embraces God's masculine design for men.

With role models like that, the next generation of men will likely emulate many of the poor examples they have observed.

You see, a young man growing up without a strong, involved mentor is just a boy seeking his identity. He may never become any more than an adolescent (in other words, somebody who has reached puberty but has never grown up). A young man under the mentorship of a noble, chival-rous man is called a *squire*. He will become a modern-day *knight*.

Today's boys may become tomorrow's wanderers.
Today's **SQUIRES** will be tomorrow's **KNIGHTS**.

So tomorrow's hope for authentic manhood is unques-tionably in *today's boys*.

However, today's boys need *changed men*.

But what is the catalyst for changing men? We will change men by convincing them *their sons* desperately need fantastic *role models* and *mentors* in their dads, coaches, Scout Masters, uncles, big brothers, teachers and any other adult males with whom the boys are in contact. We must also understand that *fatherless boys* have little hope unless other men step in to fill the void.

In the pages that follow you will find convincing portrayals of the current state of our men and boys. You will read inspiring arguments for our son's need of mentorship and training into authentic manhood. In chapter 5 you will discover an effective plan for mentoring our teen boys. And finally, I will clearly illustrate the hope realized when you touch the lives of our future men.

We must alter the current path of family breakdown, community disconnectedness, national crisis, and faith erosion. Tomorrow's *knights* are the future leaders of the family, church, community and nation. Their hope lies in "a few good men" who will raise them up; raise a generation who will serve, lead and love as God purposed.

Be their hope!

Acknowledgments

I t all started with Brian, Greg, Jimmy, Robby, Josh, Jeffrey, Wes, and Nigel. We began meeting monthly, roughing it up in the woods, roasting hotdogs over a campfire and talking about God's plan for men. Their dads and step-dads joined us (Gary, Joseph, Matt, Jerry, Darwin, Brian and Jimmy). My dad joined us. My brother, Clark, joined us – he had no sons of his own at the time. I thank them all for trying something new and for sharing their time, energy and ideas with me.

I'd also like to thank Neil Fisher for his support and mentorship. As God opened doors for me to teach parents, to write devotions and to complete this book, Neil was my sounding board. He listened and commented whenever I called on him.

Thanks, also, to my dad, Chuck Purkiss, and my brother Clark for all the proof reading and feedback they offered me throughout my new experience with writing a book.

I thank Belinda Dunn for editing my manuscript before I sent it off to the publisher.

Finally, thanks to my family. My wife, Lynn, supported and encouraged me. My daughter, Kristen, put up with a crowd of guys each month. And my son, Brian; his very existence in my life inspired me to pursue Christ-center manhood and then pass it on to him and other young men.

Chapter 1

Who Gives the Rite of Passage?

The day is warm and sultry as a distinguished crowd assembles in the grand hall of the empire's castle. At the upper end of the hall is a raised dais, upon which stands the king's throne covered with crimson satin and embroidered with lions and silver fleur-de-lis. The balcony is all aflutter with feather fans, as the ladies of the family and their attendants, who from this high place, look down upon the hall below.

The king stands before his people adorned in his formal attire and bearing the colors of the royal family. The Earl and the Count stand to each side, one clutching a battle-ready shield, the other a jousting helmet. Seated in the first two rows of the assembly, the nobles of the family give full attention to the event. Behind them, the military leaders are clad in their ceremonial uniforms, standing rigid at attention and in the order of their rank, to the number of a score or more. Beyond the guests of honor and to one side are tiers of seats for the castle gentlefolk and the guests. Upon the other side stand the burghers from the town, clothed in sober dun and russet, and yeomanry in green and brown. And in the back of this grand chamber stand two pursuivants-at-arms in tabards supporting each a splendid lance of native oak.

The whole of the great vaulted hall is full of the dull hum of many people waiting, and a ceaseless restlessness stirs the crowded throng.

A momentary hush falls as the novitiate ascends the steps of the main platform and approaches his king. This senior squire is clad in armor, new and polished to a shine of dazzling brightness, the breastplate covered with a jupon of crimson satin and embroidered with silver. His esquire-of-honor follows directly behind him bearing a sword in both hands; the cross-bearing hilt resting against his breast; the point elevated at an angle of forty-five degrees. The blade is sheathed in a crimson scabbard, and a belt of Spanish leather studded with silver bosses is wound crosswise around it. Two grave and revered knights flank the candidate and measure their steps of ascent with the lad.

The squire lowers to one knee and bows his head in humble respect. Inside, the young man is swelled up with a strange mixture of both nervous trepidation and confident assurance. As he looks up again, a warm and consoling nod from His Majesty calms this humble servant's soul.

A brief pause of motionless silence follows, and then the king brandishes the magnificent sword. In ceremonious grandeur he slowly wields the sword over the squire's head. A flash of reflective light gleams off the blade and sweeps across the chiseled walls. The monarch lowers the blade to the candidate's shoulder, pauses, then blesses the young man and formally cries in a loud voice, "Be thou a good *knight!*"

The newly appointed knight slowly erects. He turns. He faces his sponsors and friends, confident in his new identity and purpose. With fresh courage and a strength that has developed from years of training and mentorship, he is now ready to defend honor, to serve the kingdom ... and to gain favor with his lady-in-waiting.[1]

What a wonderful image of a ceremonial rite of passage. But now, look again at that mental image described above.

Look closer at that newly appointed young knight. That's *your* son in just a few short years. The knighthood commissioning described above was performed by you, *his* king. Look again; envision the future of your son's rite of passage into manhood.

Numerous cultures from the past have used ritualistic ceremony to commemorate a boy's transition into manhood, a calling-out into his new identity and purpose. This is, however, noticeably absent in our modern culture. Unfortunately, that's *not* to say that boys don't receive an initiation of some sort or another. In the absence of this rite of passage by the father, the peer group will offer a different kind of rite of passage into a different kind of manhood. The peer group offers, instead, an *initiation* into our modern culture's redefined manhood.

Before I go on, I'd like to have you ponder a question. It's a familiar question made popular on episodes of Sesame Street®. When considering a sword, a handgun, and a beer can, "Which of these three things does not belong with the others?" No, our favorite childhood show would not use these props and my illustration may seem off subject, but we'll tie it all together shortly. A sword, a handgun, and a beer can - two have obvious commonality, the other doesn't fit.

Back to the subject at hand.

MODERN RITES OF PASSAGE

Now take a different mental image of your son for a moment. Imagine him at the age of sixteen. He is out with a bunch of guys at a roadside picnic area. They are some distance from town. They have stopped at a river crossing along a winding backcountry highway. It's late on a Saturday night and your son is having the time of his life. He's sitting on the concrete, because for him, everything is spinning too fast to keep his balance. He's in a drunken stupor, his very first "drunk." He's laughing and giggling about anything and everything, including the beer being poured over his head by one of the older guys. How's this for a ceremonious initiation into manhood?

Not a pretty picture. To you, the parent, this image probably turns your stomach. But how does a teenage boy view this experience? To him, it's a milestone, an initiation into a new class among his peers. It's a "rite of passage."

It's a relief to know that this isn't something that could happen to your son; am I right? Your son hangs out with a great group of guys. He's into wholesome activities and is usually supervised by some trusting adults.

Well, I can only imagine my parents having felt the same way. They likely did not expect this sort of thing to happen to me. But, this story is actually about *my* first "drunk." Schlitz Malt Liquor®, "The sign of the bull!"

I was working as paid staff at a Boy Scout summer camp, so I was "hanging out with a great group of guys." I was an experienced Boy Scout and a camp counselor to young boys during their ultimate Scouting experience. So I was "into wholesome activities." A professional adult leadership staff ran the camp; so you can see I was "supervised by some trusting adults." From the outside looking in, my environment did not appear to promote immoral behavior, even when considering the infamous peer group influence. But I was out from under the covering of my father and I was not prepared to overcome the influence of the world.

Is this story unique? Have others faced similar encounters? As we all know the answer to be affirmative, I was blown away by a man's response to hearing this very story.

I taught this lesson in a class for parents of teen boys. While I revealed the name of the camp where my alcohol initiation took place, a gentleman began shaking his head.

He continued to shake his head and purse his lips throughout my story. It was apparent he had something to share.

His response floored me. One year prior to my experience, this gentleman worked on the staff of that very same camp. Members of the staff initiated him with beer just as I was the very next year. This is the amazing part; these coincidental stories occurred over thirty years ago. It makes me wonder if the tradition continues today.

THERE'S MORE

Have you ever seen a guy show off the small ring imprinted into the leather of his wallet? Then have him open the large pocket to retrieve some money and mistakenly pull out a packaged condom with a few small bills. He sort of shrugs it off, but lets you know that he's always ready, just in case. Then he pulls out a second condom and says that he's also ready to help out a buddy.

For some time now, losing one's virginity as a young teen has been revered as a badge of honor. Having sex brings with it a certain amount of bragging rights. For many, this defines when a guy becomes a man. The reference to one's "manhood" is even used to describe a certain body part. Steve Farrar states the antonym to this view, "In our culture, the worst thing a single man can be called is a virgin. Virgin has become a derogatory term."[2]

As a high schooler, I once attended a party that culminated in a series of claims by the guys. They each offered their experience to the group by describing their favorite position for sexual intercourse. I don't know if my silence in the conversation went unnoticed. I do recall considering those guys to be absolute liars and or fools. But to them, they were playing "one-upsmanship." They were trying to prove their manhood to their friends, their peer group. And it's unlikely their fathers ever shared with them much about sexual purity.

Steve Farrar addresses this need for the father's teaching about sexual purity:

> Proverbs is a book of teaching from father to son about gaining wisdom for life. Someone has defined wisdom as "skill in everyday living." Sex is one of the main issues in the book. Solomon wants his son to have skill in knowing how to handle his sexuality. As we read through Proverbs, the topic of sex comes up time and time again.
>
> As you read sections in Proverbs about sex, notice that the father is clear, direct, and takes the initiative. He describes sexual situations that probably will come up in his son's life, then offers the wisdom needed to handle the situation correctly. Solomon practiced preventive medicine. He wanted his son to know what steps to take in the event a tempting circumstance arose.
>
> The policy is easy to remember: *Get to your kids before their peers do!*[3]

The dilemma today is: How early do you have to get to them?

THE BACHELOR PARTY

Do you look forward to the day of your son's wedding? The day he leaves you and his mother to cleave to his wife. And, oh by the way, the day *after* his bachelor party.

How will this modern cultural event play on your son's marriage? What kind of questions will his bride suppress, afraid of the answers?

Some of us may have some stories that are better left untold. My story isn't pretty. But hear me out. Was it out of line for my friend's to bundle me up in a mattress bag and throw me in the back of a pickup truck? That's fairly harmless. How about being handcuffed? Well, now that could be a safety issue, but still no harm done. What if I was handcuffed to a keg of beer? O.K., now we're probably crossing the line. But there's more. The beer was being poured over my head (it wasn't the first time for that). I could either open my mouth and attempt to drink as fast as the beer came out, or be drenched by it. I did get the last laugh, however. I managed to get my hands on the key for the handcuffs. Having more than slightly impaired judgment by this time, I hid the key under my lower lip. I periodically loosened the handcuffs to relieve the tight grip around my wrist. Unfortunately, I eventually swallowed the key and was handcuffed to the keg of beer until it came out the other – just kidding. I didn't swallow the key. But my friends sure freaked out when I pulled the key out of my mouth at the end of the evening.

And finally, guys seem to think the bachelor party is the right time to entertain sexual immorality. It's as if the last day as a single man is the right time to partake. After all, it's culture's rite of passage ceremony; every body does it, right? Wrong! My college buddies did not take this path with my bachelor party. However, paid strippers and prostitutes are readily available to those who would pay for their services and provide them for the groom. What would *your* son's friends be willing to offer him the night before his wedding?

GANG MEMBERSHIP

It's hard to imagine a kid could become so desperate for a sense of belonging with his peer group that he would willingly take the life of another. Unfortunately, the spectrum of initiations can go to that extreme. Gang membership often becomes so important to a kid that he is willing to carry out this mandatory initiation. Some may be as benign as corner store shoplifting, others, armed robbery. And still others require a candidate to commit rape or murder. Violence and weapons are most certainly going to be involved.

BACK TO PROVERBS

King Solomon foresaw the influence of this kind of peer group on his own son. Early in the Proverbs to his son, he offers a warning. "My son, if sinners entice you, do not give in to them. ... my son, do not go along with them, do not set foot on their paths; ... Such is the end of all who go after ill-gotten gain; it takes away the life of those who get it" (Proverbs 1:10-19).

ONE OF THESE THREE THINGS...

Now let's get back to the Sesame Street question. A sword, a handgun, and a beer can. Which of these three things does not belong with the other? At first glance, two are obviously weapons; which makes the beer can the item that doesn't belong. But in light of our discussion, we can see three symbols of a rite of passage. We see the initiation by the peer group in contrast with the blessing of a father. Two are common to peer group initiations. The sword stands out as a symbol of what Robert Lewis calls a "Modern-Day Knight." It does not belong with the others.

INITIATION BY PEERS OR BLESSING BY THE FATHER

Which do you prefer, initiation by peers or blessing by the father? While the answer to this question is quite obvious, let's explore the potential consequences when a father's blessing is absent and he never calls out his son into manhood.

John Eldredge, in *Wild at Heart*, says, "Throughout the history of man given to us in Scripture, it is the father who gives the blessing and thereby 'names' the son."[4] God's plan is always the best plan. As fathers, we are to call out our sons into manhood. He goes on to say, however:

> In the case of silent, passive, or absent fathers, the question goes unanswered. "Do I have what it takes? Am I a man, Daddy?" Their silence is the answer: "I don't know ... I doubt it ... you'll have to find out for yourself ... probably not."
>
> And every wound, whether it's assaultive or passive, delivers with it a *message*.
>
> What does a boy do with that? First, I became an unruly teen. I got kicked out of school, had a police record. We often misunderstand that behavior as "adolescent rebellion," but those are the cries for involvement, for *engagement*.[5]

We're going to revisit the teen rebellion issue again later. But in the absence of initiation, boys never become men. They remain in a perpetual state of adolescence. In John Eldredge's sequel to *Wild at Heart*, *The Way of the Wild Heart*, he draws the same conclusion:

You see, what we have now is a world of uninitiated men. Partial men. Boys, mostly, walking around in men's bodies, with men's jobs and families, finances, and responsibilities. The passing on of masculinity was never completed, if it was begun at all. The boy was never taken through the process of masculine initiation. That's why most of us are Unfinished Men.[6]

INVITATION INTO MANHOOD

What if a boy is *invited* into the fellowship of men? What if he is treated like a man? He is expected to *act* like a man. Not a brute or wimpy version, but Christ-like - courage, strength, and love all wrapped into one. Can he live up to all this? Absolutely. He will still have plenty of moments acting like a child, so expect that and don't overreact to it. Just know this: kids can live up to the expectations we set for them.

Let's go to Robert Lewis' *Raising a Modern-Day Knight*. He emphasizes three critical elements for bestowing manhood, features that are typically absent today:

First, we have failed to deliver to our sons a clear, inspiring, biblically grounded *definition of manhood.*

Second, most fathers lack a *directional process* that calls their sons to embrace the manhood they should be able to define.

A third shortcoming involves the loss of *ceremony.*[7]

Dr. Lewis' reference to the loss of ceremony is obviously the topic of this opening chapter. And the issues of a "definition of manhood" and "directional process" will be addressed in detail later. But let us first look to scripture for some ideas for a rite of passage ceremony.

THE RITE OF PASSAGE FOR JESUS

Why is it that we refer to God as the Father and Jesus, the Son of God? To be honest, I'm not sure I can offer a qualified answer, but I do know this: *we*, as fathers, can draw from this model for our own relationship with *our* sons.

Matthew 3 provides us with an excellent model for our discussion on the rite of passage. To begin the story, John the Baptist points out that "the kingdom of heaven is near." He then introduces the event that was prophesied by Isaiah: "Prepare the way for the Lord, make straight paths for him." John goes on to declare, "He will baptize you with the Holy Spirit and with fire." Very little of this made sense to those present at the time. But God, the Father, soon makes a grand entry as he carries out the rite of passage for Jesus, His Son. We'll find that even John did not fully understand what was about to happen.

When Jesus arrives, John's confusion is revealed. It doesn't make sense to him that Jesus, the Messiah, came to be baptized by him, a mere prophet. When Jesus states, "Let it be so now; it is proper for us to do this to fulfill all righteousness." Well, what could John say? "Then John consented."

Consented!? Of course he consented. He was introducing the Savior of the world. That would be like a seventeen year old challenging his father about curfew. O.K., bad example. But John did what he had to do.

At this point the Father carries out a ceremonial rite of passage. He calls out His Son into ministry and publicly blesses Him. And this is where we, as fathers, can draw from His example.

We see in this story all the elements of a good ceremony. Robert Lewis lays them out for us in *Raising a Modern-Day Knight*. They include:

21

First, *memorable ceremonies are costly.*
Second, *memorable ceremonies ascribe value.*
Third, *memorable ceremonies employ symbols.*
Finally, and perhaps most important, *memorable ceremonies empower a life with vision.*[8]

We've already seen the process that led up to this event. John the Baptist was prophesied to be the one to "prepare the way for the Lord." God ordained the miraculous conception of John for this purpose. John lived his entire life in preparation for this event. When Dr. Lewis says, *"memorable ceremonies are costly,"* this ceremony cost John his life; literally speaking - his head was served on a platter.

Next, the heavens open, the Spirit of God descends as a dove, lighting on Jesus. About this time I'll bet John the Baptist was glad he did what he was told. Then God, the Father, announces, "This is my Son, whom I love; with him I am well pleased."

The Father has *"ascribed value"* to His Son by declaring His love for Jesus and His feelings about Jesus. This expression of love from father to son is vital. Before you read any further, you must read Dr. Lewis' stories on pages 28 and 35 of *Raising a Modern-Day Knight.* My eyes well up with tears every time I read them - at least four times now.

The Father *"employed symbols"* as the Spirit of God descended like a dove and was a light on Jesus. We see these two symbols, the dove and the light, still today in the church.

Finally, the Father *"empowered a life with vision."* Jesus went on to overcome the temptations of Satan. He began preaching the gospel and healing the sick. Jesus had to know what his purpose was in order to fulfill it. He later proclaimed to a crowd, "I must preach the good news of the kingdom of God to the other towns also, because that is why I was sent" (Luke 4:43). And Matthew 4:23 gives us a clear description of His ministry: "Jesus went throughout Galilee, teaching in their synagogues, preaching the good news of the kingdom, and healing every disease and sickness among the people." Jesus' mission concluded with the ultimate fulfillment of prophecy; Jesus became the instrument of the new covenant. As he explained to his disciples, "For even the Son of Man did not come to be served, but to serve, and to give His life a ransom for many" (Mark 10:45). The Father empowered His Son for this purpose.

Wow! That's a ceremony never to be outdone! But it gives us dads a model to emulate. These four elements of ceremony can set a course for our sons that will help them overcome temptation and find God's will for *their* purpose in life.

"Where there is no vision, the people are unrestrained..." (Proverbs 29:18).

SYMBOLS FOR RITE OF PASSAGE

We see several symbols used in the story above. The two I've already mentioned are the dove and the light. We also see the water used for the baptism and a reference to Jesus baptizing with the Holy Spirit and with fire.

I did not choose any of these symbols for my son's rite of passage into manhood. I had read a number of books relating to mentoring boys and found a common theme. The cover design of five different books depicted a *sword* on the front cover. *Raising a Modern-Day Knight* was one of them. It was an easy choice.

I also love the scriptural description of the armor of God in Ephesians 6. With the emphasis I place on teaching boys the truths of God's word, the "sword of the Spirit, which is the word of God," has wonderful symbolism for this purpose.

But let me warn you, don't go cheap. As Robert Lewis prescribed: memorable ceremonies are costly. I wouldn't pick up a seven-dollar letter-opener shaped as a small replica sword. Picture the look on your son's face as you solemnly present this little trinket to him, reach for symbolism from thin air and come up empty. Your young lad may likely snicker under his breadth and your good intentions may result in a total embarrassment.

I spent $150 on a replica medieval Crusader sword. Similar swords can be purchased for prices ranging from $45 to $350. The weapon I chose is heavy and sharp. It has the appearance of hand made construction. And it looks as if it had been shaped using crude techniques from the sixteenth century. Finally, it bears the Crusader's cross on the end of the handle.

I'll explain later how I presented the sword on my son's thirteenth birthday. But since then, a number of other men have joined me in our endeavor to mentor our boys. We have also reached out to several boys lacking a male role model in their lives. They have all seen my son's sword and the symbolism it represents. When a number of the men approached me about acquiring swords for their boys, I pursued a group discount for a volume order. As a result, we committed to present each of the boys with a sword. This presentation will occur when each of them is ready to go out on his own, equipped to be a Godly man. So we ordered an additional fifteen swords (warranting a 10% volume discount!). Awesome! I mean for the swords, not the discount.

The sky is the limit as you search for ideas regarding rite of passage symbols. Robert Lewis and his friends designed a family crest, then had it printed and framed. They also had the crest custom made onto gold rings for themselves and each of the seven boys under their mentorship. A friend of mine has a different idea. He presented each of his boys with a hunting rifle on their thirteenth birthday.

Let's take a look at God's word now. Read His exhortations to mentors, His push for teaching with a generational vision:

> "Now this is the commandment, the statutes and the judgments which the Lord your God has commanded me to teach you, that you might do them in the land where you are going over to possess it, so that you and your son and your grandson might fear the Lord your God... (Deuteronomy 6:1-2, NASB).
>
> You shall love the Lord your God with all your heart and with all your soul and with all your might. These words, which I am commanding you today, shall be on your heart. You shall teach them diligently to your sons and you shall talk of them when you sit in your house and when you walk by the way and when you lie down and when you rise up (Deuteronomy 6:5-7, NASB).
>
> But the plans of the Lord stand firm forever, the purposes of his heart through all generations (Psalm 33:11).

What far-reaching value and powerful vision for us all!

CEREMONIES

As we continue, I refer you again to *Raising a Modern-Day Knight*. If you have not already read Dr. Lewis' entire book, I highly recommend it. The book puts much emphasis on the topic of ceremony and will serve you well. "Ceremonies are those special occasions that weave the fabric of human existence. Weddings. Award banquets. Graduations. The day you became an Eagle Scout or were accepted into a fraternity. *We remember because of ceremony.*"[9] An example of a current day manhood ceremony is seen in the Jewish Bar Mitzvah. I know little about this ceremony, but I fully understand the significance and value of such a ceremony. By the age of twelve or thirteen, a boy is becoming a man and must be invited into manhood.

My first attempt at something similar was, well, just plain weak. I put all my forethought into the *symbol*; this included extensive brainstorming, then research, then shopping (via the internet). By the time my son's thirteenth birthday came, I must have run out of creative juices. So, with a large group of family members present, I pulled out this handsome sword and briefly explained its purpose. I talked about the significance of the remaining years of my influence on him as he entered manhood. I also talked about the symbolic representation of the sword for this endeavor. But I found myself short of appropriate words and experienced a moment of awkward silence.

Three years later, my wife and I did a similar presentation to my daughter with a cross pendant. This time, I learned and expanded from my first attempt at this with my son. I asked all of the family members to prepare a blessing and or prayer for her. I put my daughter in a chair in front of all in attendance. I explained the significance of the teen years as she grows and matures. I presented the cross pendant. I read numerous scriptures that illustrated the symbolic features of the pendant design. Each family member then had an opportunity to offer his or her blessing and prayer for my daughter. I then closed in prayer. This time, no shortage of words, no awkward silence; we accomplished what we had purposed.

With so few men today having experienced their own calling out from their fathers, and with so many absentee and work-a-holic fathers today, the next generation of men may be lost in their pursuit for manhood. Or, I should say, even more lost than *our* generation. I believe it is critical for us to fulfill God's plan by carrying out ceremonious rites of passage for our sons, as well as for the fatherless boys in our circle of influence. And let us look beyond the next generation. Let us see the generational legacy of this endeavor.

Chapter 2

Dad vs. Culture

S*tar Wars* - Luke Skywalker - Darth Vader. We all know the story. And I'm sure we're all familiar with the haunting sound of Darth Vader's labored breathing. The villain of *Star Wars* requires that ominous mask as a sort-of life-support device. Somehow that apparatus affects his breathing. Oh how that sound bite has been replayed: "Luuuke," ... *inhale* ... "I am your faaatherrr," ... *exhale*.

But how about the history of this man? The story of his turn to evil was eventually revealed in another episode – *Star Wars Episode II, Attack of the Clones.* Young Anakin Skywalker is discovered as having the natural skills and talents of the Jedi Knight. He is recruited as an apprentice under the mentorship of an experienced Jedi, Obi-Wan Kenobi. The young man learns the skills of the Jedi quickly and occasionally displays an aptitude that surpasses his mentor. As is not uncommon with extremely talented young men, Anakin gets cocky. He begins to resent his status as a protégé.

If you're familiar with the story, you may remember this scene. Anakin is left alone to protect the beautiful Senator Padmc' Amidala. She offers him a compliment:

Padme': You've grown up.

Anakin: Master Obi-Wan manages not to see it.
Don't get me wrong. Obi Wan is a great master. As wise as Master Yoda. As powerful as Master Windu.
I am truly thankful to be his apprentice. In some ways, a lot of ways, I'm really ahead of him. I'm ready for the trials. But he feels that I'm too unpredictable! HE WON'T LET ME MOVE ON!

Padme': That must be frustrating.

Anakin: It's worse! He's overly critical. He never listens. He, he doesn't understand. IT'S NOT FAIR!

Padme': All mentors have a way of seeing more of our faults than we would like. It's the only way we grow.

Anakin: I know.[1]

You can see the attitude of Anakin's heart. And if you watch the teenage boys today, you'll see that this same outlook is prevalent. The name we use for this phenomenon, teen rebellion, has even lost its sting. We've come to expect, accept, and even ignore this in our teenagers, especially our sons. And when allowed to progress to an extreme, we see outbursts like the one at Columbine High School in Littleton, Colorado. Similarly, this mind-set ultimately drags our Star Wars movie character to the "Dark Side."

"MY YOUNG PADAWAN"

I won't try to portray "The Force" in *Star Wars* as analogous with our omnipotent God and the "Dark Side" as Satan. The storyline fails to illustrate the grace given us through the sacrifice of our Lord, Jesus Christ. I'm drawing analogy only from the relationship of Jedi and padawan, mentor and protégé, *knight* and *squire*. I'm using the rebellious nature of Anakin Skywalker as an illustration of our son's rebellious nature.

Notice, however, there is more that makes this analogy so pertinent with today's challenges for fathers of growing and maturing boys. There is an interesting commonality with Anakin, the apprentice, and today's male youth. Their egos are being fed by Satan and the world just as they discover a natural desire for independence. They realize they can make their own decisions and choices; they have their own ideas and values. Even if their values are in line with their father's teachings, they want to take ownership of them.

Two more scenes in this movie illustrate contemporary trends among our teen boys. First, the leader of the evil forces, Supreme Chancellor Palpatine, implores Anakin. He does it just as Satan and today's culture do with our own boys:

> "You don't need guidance, Anakin. In time, you will learn to trust your feelings. Then you will be invincible."[2]

How's that for a secular world-view – the typical feel good, relativism of today's culture? And the Jedi masters recognize Anakin's response to these lies:

> Obi Wan: He has much to learn, master. His abilities have made him, well, arrogant.

Yoda: Yes, yes. A flaw more and more common among
Jedi. Hmm. Too sure of them selves, they are.[3]

"THE THING-IN-A-BOX"

I began meeting monthly with a group of men and boys
when my son was thirteen years old. To instill a sense of
purpose for the group, I introduced the group's plan with
an illustration. I contrasted the same images from Anakin's
training into Jedi Knighthood with a medieval squire's
training to become a knight.

I conspicuously revealed a long cardboard box. When
asked, I refused to disclose its contents. The boys began
referring to the mysterious contents as "the thing-in-a-
box." Later, I dramatically wielded from the box a toy light
saber, similar to the one used by the *Star Wars* Jedi knight.
I described the rebellious nature of Anakin Skywalker and
explained that, like Anakin, teenagers tend to rebel against
their mentors and other authorities. Anakin ultimately gave
in to the "Dark Side." I then ceremoniously brandished my
son's Crusader Sword from the box. I explained that our
group's purpose for meeting regularly was to help counter
this rebellious nature and bring the boys up into manhood,
resisting the barriers of rebellion. To this day, the boys still
refer to the sword as "the thing-in-a-box."

TEEN REBELLION

For some reason, our culture has decided that teen
rebellion is normal, unavoidable, and even acceptable. We
joke about it and make light of it. The dynamics between
authority and rebellion portrayed by Obi-Wan and Anakin
are accepted as just the way it is.

I say there is a better way. So let's take a look at "Dad
vs. Culture." Let's look at how God sees rebellion and how

the relationship/authority dynamics can play on this issue, specifically with teenage boys. Let's discover the deceit of culture as it relates to the parent/teen relationship.

MANKIND'S ETHOS OF REBELLION

If there was ever a recurring theme for God's chosen people, it would be their propensity to rebel against Him. The original sin in the garden – rebellion against God. Idol worship at the base of Mount Sinai– rebellion against God. Lack of trust to enter the Promised Land – rebellion against God. Peter's denial of Jesus – rebellion against God. As scripture reveals over and over again: "…you rebelled against the command of the Lord your God. You grumbled … you did not trust in the Lord your God" (Deuteronomy 1:26-32).

The original sin by Adam and Eve is worth a closer look. Genesis 3:1-7 tells the story. "Now the serpent was more crafty than any of the other wild animals…" So he preyed on the one more easily deceived. "'You will not surely die,' the serpent said to the woman … the fruit of the tree was good for food and pleasing to the eye, and also desirable for gaining wisdom…" So the woman gave in to the temptation. Commentary on this passage often highlights that "her husband, … was with her…" then ate the fruit. Because he is the one who received God's commandment regarding the tree, he is the one responsible for the obedience. He was the one given authority and failed to stand firm on behalf of the woman. Was he not listening as Eve was tempted by Satan? Maybe he was watching ESPN and missed the whole thing. Ya, that's it, he missed it all.

But the Lord took this rebellion seriously. The penalty for the original sin is death. The penalty for the rebellious Jews was the law of the old covenant.

REBELLIOUS SONS

It's a scary thought to consider God's law as it applied to a rebellious son of the Old Testament. "If a man has a stubborn and rebellious son ... bring him to the elders at the gate ... Then all the men of his town shall stone him to death" (Deuteronomy 21:18-19). Thank God for the grace of the new covenant – we are no longer "under the law." We can offer grace to *our* sons. We can love our sons as we nurture and grow in relationship with them, just as God does with His children.

Even King David recognized his own youthful disobedience. As he says in Psalm 25:7, "Remember not the sins of my youth and my rebellious ways." Here, a man after God's own heart had to repent the sins of his youth and his rebellious ways. But truly, why would we expect any different?

And how about one of today's Christian giants? Dr. James Dobson relates a story in his book *Bringing Up Boys*. He tells of a day when his mother had to call his dad, a traveling evangelist, and tell him, "I need you." You see, at age sixteen our beloved Dr. Dobson was getting a bit smart with his mom. And at the first sign of his disrespect to her, his dad literally gave up his career to be around during those last two volatile years. The good news is Dr. Dobson's father was willing to make the sacrifice to be closer to home. Through a commitment to relationship with his son, Dr. Dobson's dad finished raising young James into the man we know today, by the grace of God.[6]

Yes, by the grace of God. You see, *God* instituted the family as His principal instrument of relationship and authority. He established the relationships between husband and wife, parent and child, father and son. From these relationships we are to practice our responsibilities with authority, submission, teaching and learning. And it is here we deal with youthful rebellion.

While scripture tells us, "Children, obey your parents in the Lord, for this is right" (Ephesians 6:1-2), Jesus also warned his disciples "children will rebel against their parents" (Matthew 10:21). So King David and Dr. Dobson would not have been exempt from this youthful attribute. But we must understand that "he who rebels against the authority is rebelling against what God has instituted" (Romans 13:2).

THE ADOLESCENT BRAIN

A number of brain developmental processes are occurring during adolescence, which may help explain some of the irrational behavior of teens. These neural changes are quite influential in the choices teens make and can drive a parent crazy. Both boys and girls experience these changes.

Most significantly, the teenage brain takes on a second dramatic period of growth and accelerates the pruning of unused neural connections. As a result, the adolescent often struggles with normal thinking and decision-making. In addition, most of this growth occurs in the frontal lobe, which is commonly referred to as the "judgment center" of the brain. So imagine your teenager with an uncharted desire for independence and combining it with a difficulty in controlling impulses and weighing risks. You may begin to recognize the need for a little understanding when you observe what appears to be a brain-dead, rebellious young adult. Making the point very well, Blaine Bartel dedicates an entire chapter titled "I'm a Little Brain-Damaged, So Get Used to It," in his book *Let Me Tell You What Your Teens Are Telling Me*.[4]

CAUGHT IN BETWEEN

I mentioned a teen's uncharted desire for independence. As physical adults, our older teens are appropriately ready for some freedom and autonomy. In fact, they are a bit out of place as dependents under our authority. Every culture other than the modern high tech cultures of today has or had fifteen and sixteen year olds marrying, having babies and making a living. Only today's technologically advanced society all but requires these young adults to stay at home while continuing their advanced education. This subculture of sixteen to nineteen year olds is caught between childhood and adulthood. That sounds like a rock and hard place to me. This no-man's-land puts a huge strain on parent-child relationships. And I'm not sure if there is a fix; it seems universal that parents and older teens have conflict.

But despair not. This phase is temporary. Expect it. Don't over-react to it. Be cool, calm and collected. Not that I pulled this off very well myself, but I believe you can do better. And when (not if, but when) you find yourself screaming and flailing like you've lost all control (I've been there), just take a deep breath, pray for grace and wisdom, then apologize to your teen and move forward. Mr. Bartel's very next chapter to parents is titled: "Quit Trying to Act Perfect Because It's Obvious That You're Not."[5]

I recommend you read at least six books about raising teenagers. After the first two, you may not be convinced. By the time you've read four books, you'll figure there must be something to what they're saying. If you read at least six, you'll finally be convinced (you think I'm joking). The teaching on this is quite consistent. Your natural parental responses to the phenomenon of teenagedom probably won't work. We all could use the help of someone who's either been there and/or from someone with a professional background in the area. I've done a lot of both.

TEACH RESPECT AND SELF-CONTROL

So what's to be done? Let me suggest first that we are to teach our children to respect authority. Respect should be taught at a young age and it starts with respect for the authority of parents. Few of our kids today are properly trained in this area. We must teach appropriate obedience: immediate, complete, correct, without complaint, and without challenge. "Without challenge" still allows for respectful appeals; however, explanations by parents are not obligatory. If kids become accustomed to an explanation for every parental decision, they are likely to begin evaluating the merit of our decisions and then expect answers that meet their young perspective. Parents should seldom offer explanations to the very young. Then, as the kids get older, offer explanations according to their ability to understand. But remember, explanations are still at the parents' discretion.

While respect also applies to babysitters, teachers, policemen, and adults in general, the family home is the practice field and the father is the coach. "For I have chosen him, so that he will direct his children and his household after him to keep the way of the Lord by doing what is right and just" (Genesis 18:19). And just as an elder of the church must "manage his own family well and see that his children obey him with proper respect" (1 Timothy 3:4), all fathers should strive for this noble family attribute.

Next, we are to teach self-control. Our kids must learn at an early age that their desires will not drive the lives of everyone around them. The "all about me" mentality of today's culture will not be tolerated. They will frequently be denied what they want and they are to accept this fact of life without complaint. They will not always get candy when they want it, they may have to share their favorite toy, they may even have to eat their vegetables. You may require them to turn off the TV. GASP! Computer and phone use may not be permitted in the privacy of their bedroom.

Men, scripture says we are to "encourage the young men to be self-controlled" (Titus 2:6). We can share with our sons just as the elders of old did to the young men: "Be self-controlled and alert. ... Resist him [Satan], standing firm in the faith, ... And the God of all grace ... will himself restore you and make you strong..." (1Peter 5:8-10).

Now, consistency is paramount. It bolsters effective parental enforcement by establishing and maintaining precedence. Being consistent also makes it easier for you to stay calm and collected when responding to obedience issues. Inconsistency breeds contempt and makes you out to be the bad guy when enforcement takes place.

Respect, obedience, self-control – easier said than done. The culture says, "If it feels good, do it." "If it's right for you, it can't be wrong." This relativism tempts our kids. They are tugged in different directions. They must have a foundation on which to stand. That foundation is, of course, Jesus Christ.

Jesus is the Word (John 1:1), He is the truth, He is the way (John 14:6). Jesus trusted the truth of the Word and He looked to *His* Father for guidance. He is our example.

Luke 4:1-13 tells the story of Jesus' strength against temptation, His trust in the Word and His trust in His Father. While Jesus was vulnerable in the wilderness, Satan tempted Him three times. Each time Jesus responded by quoting scripture. We all know the outcome. Jesus prevailed and "When the devil had finished all his tempting, he left him until an opportune time." And this is an important pattern of Satan for which we fathers must be aware – *an opportune time*. An opportune time for tempting teenagers is any time they are not asleep. So as we "encourage the young men to be self-controlled," we must teach from the Word. We must give them the scriptural truths that will guide their hearts to obedience and repentance. In fact, that brings us full circle to the knighthood training and the sword from Chapter 1: the "*Sword* of the Spirit, which is the *word* of God" and

38

a weapon of the "full armor of God" (Ephesians 6:17, 11, *italics mine*).

Dads, we must be a protective covering over our sons (and daughters) during their most vulnerable years! We must emulate the Father/son relationship of God the Father and Jesus, the Son. We must relate with our children as foretold in Luke chapter 1: "And he will go on before the Lord, in the spirit and power of Elijah, *to turn the hearts of the fathers to their children*, and the disobedient to the wisdom of the righteous – to make ready a people prepared for the Lord" (vs. 17, *italics mine*). Our heart for our children must abound! We must balance our position of authority over our children with a loving relationship that can suppress their natural rebellion. Later in this chapter I'll introduce a phrase coined by Josh McDowell that will solidify this idea. But the bottom line is, our heart for them must prevail over our - get ready for this - our bent to be legalistic behavior-enforcing disciplinarians, our standing as prideful self-image-protecting perfectionists, or our trait as selfish identity-wielding careerists. Think about these modern-man reputations. "All of it is meaningless, a chasing after the wind" (Ecclesiastes 2:17).

The impact of fathers blundering with their sons (and daughters) is reflected in this: "We expect Modern-Day Knights to somehow emerge from the homes of absent or irresponsible fathers – men whose lives are marked by workaholism, selfishness, and absenteeism. ... Everyone in medieval society knew that the sons of peasants did not become knights. In modern society, neither do the sons of absent or irresponsible dads."[7]

MODERN CULTURE

What is it that we must stand against in today's modern culture? Let me offer some personal observations. I offer these insights following considerable biblical research and extensive reading from contemporary Christian authors. But, while a social science professional may have a research team at his disposal and a database of statistics at his fingertips, my purpose here is merely to help you observe and consider for yourself. You're going to accept or reject, not based on my credibility or the credibility of my evidence, but on your own related assessment of culture around you. So let's see if we are in agreement.

THE FAMILY vs. CULTURE

My first point is summed up by Robert Lewis: "There was a time in America when family values were reinforced by the culture, but that time is long past."[8] Art Linkletter has a similar view. He wrote the Forward for a book written by S. Truet Cathy, founder of Chick-fil-a. In this book entitled: *"It's Better to Build Boys Than Mend Men*, Mr. Linkletter has this to say: "Never before in the history of Western civilization has a generation of children been subjected to such an avalanche of vulgarity, violence, drug abuse, and sexual promiscuity."[9] We must recognize that the times, "they are a-changin." The people of our nation have been moving away from God-fearing faith. With our loss of biblical values, we have seen family disintegration, moral decay, political corruption, etc., etc., etc. Although I see in our nation signs of a turn back to God, a significant minority (if not a small majority) of our population is taking a hard left, severing itself from the Truth. As described in Romans chapter 1, they "suppress the truth by their wickedness, since what may be known about God is plain to them, because God has made it plain to them. For since the creation of the world God's invisible attributes, his eternal power and divine nature - have been clearly seen, being understood from what has been made, so that men are without excuse" (vs. 18-20). We must be keenly aware of this deceit, attentive to every aspect of the lies that come from this denial of God's truth. "The heart of the wise inclines to the right, but the heart of the fool to the left" (Ecclesiastes 10:2).

We're going to look at five different areas of cultural influence on family life. We will see that each may be countering the values we seek for our kids. Some are equally a threat to our daughters, but many have an unbalanced harmful effect on our sons. These areas of interest include the "rat race," the school system, the media, the peer group, and finally, the church.

TIME MANAGEMENT

In today's rat race, or "routine panic" as James Dobson calls it, we are in a never-ending fight for time with our family. Each family member is being pulled in so many directions; we must be made of elastic to stretch in all directions without being torn. Unfortunately, the less pliable get ripped apart.

Because our work place is no longer collocated with or near the home as in days past, employment takes dads and many moms away from the home for a majority of our time. Add to that, our pursuit of professional success requires a forty-plus hour workweek, with the commute, business trips, over-time, on-call status, and other work-related time robbers. This careerism robs us of any real quantity or quality family time. A simple look at our pocket calendar, or palm pilot, shows the imbalance of our focus. We squeeze family time into the small portions of leftover time, often giving it only a token effort.

The typical academic and extra-curricular schedule of a student looks no different than that of the employed parents. Their day also includes a forty-plus hour school week; with field trips, homework, athletic or band practice, Boy Scout troop meetings, student government, ROTC, Chess Club, and – I know I'm leaving something out. Even if the parents were independently wealthy with all the free time in the world, their kids may not have time for them.

Then there's what my dad called the "boob-tube." I'm sure you've seen the results of studies; the stats speak for themselves. We are all glued to the TV. The accumulation of hours in front of the TV resembles the accumulation of dollars in the national debt; the numbers are so big they loose all meaning. One study I can't verify (remember, no research team) concluded that a child will spend more time in front of a TV by age six than he will his entire life with his dad. Ouch! My family's TV is hooked up to the VCR and DVD only. No local, cable or satellite TV.

We're going to look at the issue of content on TV media shortly. But let's look at another video monitor attraction.

The computer may not replace the TV as an expensive time sifter. No, it's only adding to the cost. With video games, instant messaging, e-mail, blogs, and who-knows-what-will-be-invented-next, we are face-to-face with the computer screen more often than we are each other. I dare you to log the hours at the computer for each family member. It'll scare you.

Now let's look at media exposure for kids. Last year's statistics tell us that our kids are tied to the media (TV, computer, video games, etc.) almost 45 hours per week.[10] That's over six hours a day. This trend is even partially credited for our nation's obesity problem.

James Dobson, in *Bringing Up Boys*, says, "The harried lifestyle that characterizes most Westerners leads not only to the isolation of people from each other in the wider community; it is also the primary reason for the breakdown of the family. Husbands and wives have no time for each other and many of them hardly know their children." He shares that "the lives of each family member are usually so jam-packed that the opportunity to spend time together doing unique activities - talking about life, visiting special places, playing games, and sharing spiritual explorations - has to be scheduled in advance. Few do so."[11] As I said earlier, boys can suffer more than girls. Dr. Dobson goes on to say, "...the trouble we are having with our children is linked directly to routine panic and the increasing isolation and detachment from you, their parents. Furthermore, boys typically suffer more from these conditions than do girls. Why? Because boys are more likely to get off-course when they are not guided and supervised carefully. They are inherently more volatile and less stable emotionally. They flounder in chaotic, unsupervised, and undisciplined circumstances."[12] Thank you, Dr. Dobson, for your insight!

It's a simple argument. Our culture says professional success and money are the ultimate goals. Get them at all costs. God says, "Whoever loves money never has money enough; whoever loves wealth is never satisfied with his income. This too is meaningless" (Ecclesiastes 5:10).

SCHOOL

We have already hammered the issue of time spent at school. I have also shared the idea that parents are to be the protective covering over children during their vulnerable years. Yet we trust this responsibility to a delegated surrogate parent, the teacher. I so appreciate the teacher whose heart goes out to the students; my sister and brother-in-law are such teachers. But, though many of these professional educators have your child's best interest in mind, you can't assume that. Even the best of them can offer only so much in a one to twenty or thirty teacher to student ratio. Much of their time focuses on crowd control or the misbehavior issues of a small minority.

All school districts mandate requirements into their curriculum. I don't have a problem with that. However, we as a nation mistakenly believe these mandates must forbid religious teaching. The Northwest Ordinance of 1789, a law written by our Founding Fathers, set forth the requirements of statehood for prospective territories. This law once *required* encouragement of religion as necessary for schools and the means of education.[13] This ordinance has mysteriously disappeared from the law books. But so has a large amount of our nation's Christian religious values. In fact, the Supreme Court had been officially declaring the U.S. a "Christian nation" or a "religious people" for over 175 years, then suddenly reversed precedence with a minority liberal agenda in the 1940's and 50's. Many school districts, if not most, now require politically correct values training with *intolerance* to our Christian heritage. This mandated instruction is no longer rooted in a biblical worldview. The associated dilemma for the Christian family has been escalating rapidly with years of liberal court decisions.

I would also like to suggest that the school system has been forced to "teach to the test." Government accountability of schools has created this problem. Test-taking skills and goals have taken the front seat over the love of learning. Test answers now prevail over critical thinking skills. Knowledge is the end goal, while wisdom is reserved only for the aged.

Today's pursuit of education prepares our youngsters to be employees, answering to a boss, counting on company entitlements that hopefully surpass government entitlements. The entrepreneur must buck the system to break free of this mentality. The financially savvy must resist dependence on the company medical and retirement plan or Social Security and Medicare.

The most alarming issues of the education system are illustrated by the story of Carol Everette. She travels across the country sharing her testimony. She once envisioned a multi-million dollar industry created by her manipulations within the school system. She developed a sex ed curriculum and began teaching it in her local public schools. Her motive: generate future clients for her growing abortion business, ultimately making her rich. She created a business model centered on two things: introduce the minds of elementary students with thoughts of sex while demeaning the authority and credibility of the parents. She was on the road to success until she responded to God's call and accepted Jesus as her Lord.

I hate to say it, but the noble cause of public education is as much a victim of the cultural left as the family. Even the homosexual agenda is successfully infiltrating our schools. We want so much to make it work, our politicians just keep pouring more money into the system. But I believe the fix comes from Christian family oversight of the system. It also requires a court system that respects the nations historic values rather than today's self-oriented immoral values.

THE MEDIA

I can't tell if TV emulates the culture or if the culture emulates TV. What came first, the chicken or the egg, the sitcom characters' behavior or the pop culture behavior? I tend to think the power of the media often determines the direction of our youth behavior. Our kids (and young adults) are so connected with the characters on TV and the actors' lives portrayed in the tabloids, they actually emulate the behavior (or misbehavior) of the fictitious as well as the real (although I wouldn't call Hollywood the real world). Have you noticed that most female characters are beautiful and dominating and that most male characters are goofy and sex crazed? Women's clothes reveal every curve of their body and expose key body parts. The guys are either good-looking and dumb or ugly and dumb. The great thing is the humor is hilarious. The sad thing is – the humor is hilarious. Picking on the male gender has gotten to be so prominent in TV humor; we're now accepting the role TV has defined for us. But humor has a way of revealing reality. So again, what came first, the chicken or the egg?

And how about the content on TV. I just saw a newspaper article entitled: "Sex, Drugs, and Disfuntionality star on cable TV." Now there's a good reason to avoid the television.

Then we have the TV commercials. They are just more of the same. Especially when the product of the advertisement is beer and the commercial break is during a football game. Then the girls are even more dominant and beautiful while the guys are even more dumb and sex crazed.

Can we hope for any different on the big screen? Actually, we can. They are hard to find, but I've seen some wonderful stories told in some recent movies. They are portraying men as decent and noble. But again, you have to look hard, because the majority, especially the comedies, still like to pick on the guys.

Our next media category is music. With the contemptible values represented on MTV, consider the fact that it owns more than fifty channels in twenty-eight languages and 168 countries.[14] I understand that at one point it was the most watched network worldwide. The music industry continues to draw notoriety with its sin-centered themes, most notably, implicit, immoral sex. And the youthful audience is enormous. The necessary alarm for parents should come from the following extreme example. I watched an interview of a drag-queen music artist. With his low, but feminine voice, he announced, "I usually like to destroy the minds of children." While he is only one extreme example, I fear an abundance of subtle and some not-so-subtle mental influences result from the lyrics and images portrayed in today's music. To counter all this, it is exciting to see the current contemporary Christian music explosion.

I will once again go to Dr. Dobson to help me sum this all up. As stated in an ad for his *Bringing Up Boys Videos*, "The degradation of men in the media directly affects boys. It confuses boys about what it means to be a boy, a man, a father, a husband. Parents need to defend their boys and teach them their God-given roles, despite what culture says."[15]

THE PEER GROUP

It's official. I think we all know this deep down, but we don't want to believe it. The peer group is the strongest influence on our youth today.[16] Dr. Kevin Leman explains, "Moms and dads of teenagers quickly discover that their children pay much more attention to the opinions and ideas of their schoolmates and friends than they do what they hear at home."[17] The least qualified source for life's ideals and principles has taken over the training role. The peer group influence is stronger than that of teachers, coaches, Scout Masters, Sunday school teachers; and it's even stronger than the influence of parents. I'd venture to say, it's often stronger than all of them combined.

Remember when we recognized earlier in this chapter the rebellious nature of youth? Consider also the foolish perspective they tend to have when dealing with life's issues. Then recognize the product of young adults produced by this self-trained subpopulation. "He who walks with the wise grows wise, but the companion of fools suffers harm" (Proverbs 13:20) and "Bad company corrupts good character" (1 Corinthians 15:33). Two truths that say it all.

THE CHURCH

Today's church youth group is a popular safe-haven for our kids. They are put in a setting of peers, under the roof of the church. Today's youth directors are young, energetic and often "cool." The teens are comfortable and open in this venue. These ingredients can offer our youth an experience of spiritual growth and maturity.

All of these perspectives, however, require certain assumptions. It assumes that the church peer group will be a positive influence on our kids. It assumes that the cool youth director is spiritually mature, has a strong biblical world-view and supports parental authority and family unity in the messages being taught. These assumptions, unfortunately, cannot be taken for granted.

As I said earlier, God created the family unit to be the center of learning, growing and maturing. Outsourcing this responsibility to the church youth group puts us outside God's plan. Church service attendance should not depart from this family model. I highly encourage you to sit together as a family during church services. This plan reinforces the status of the family in the church and avoids the disruptions of unsupervised youngsters grouped together in the pews. If you establish this norm early and stand by it, you'll get less resistance from your kids later. This plan, however, does not preclude you from joining your kids' friends' family in the church pews.

Consider my previous reference to the youth director's support of parental authority and family unity. After reading a church bulletin recently, my wife noticed the following statement, "If you are under eighteen years old and are sitting with your parents in the church sanctuary, you are in the wrong place." It then went on to explain that "Youth" is the place to be. The bulletin ad suggested that Youth Group attendance should replace church service attendance. I believe Youth Group, if attended at all, should *supplement* and *support* family worship and discipleship, not replace it.

HOW ARE WE DOING, DADS?

Sadly, we're not doing so good, guys. Dave Simmons sums it up quite well:

> Parenthood became a franchise industry. Child raising became a joint venture between parents and outside institutions – the bear-and-share theory. The schools took over value clarification and taught situational ethics. The media preempted amusement and desensitized and androgenized the children. The government shuffled them into numbers and dealt them into quotas. The legal and psychiatric literature rendered them guiltless and nonresponsible.[18]

Dads, hear this: statistic after statistic points to two realities. First, dads' involvement (or lack of) in the lives of their children (and wives) is extremely influential in the overall wellbeing of the family unit and individual family members. When men are physically or mentally *abusive*, the family suffers immensely. When men are physically *absent*, the family still suffers dramatically. And even when men are just *mentally* absent, the whole family (statistics show) is aching for his involvement. The blessings of God's design are negated. The positive side of this data concludes: a family thrives under the leadership of a morally strong and involved man. Too few families realize this blessing.

The second reality centers specifically on the father/son relationship. If it makes sense that boys should model themselves after their dads (some amazingly challenge that concept), then the health of our boys reflects the health of the father/son relationships. It's heartbreaking, though, to see the statistical data on boys' social and mental problems as compared to their female counterparts. Hey dads, what's up with that?

From James Dobson: "Boys, when compared to girls, are six times more likely to have learning disabilities, three times more likely to be registered drug addicts, and four times more likely to be diagnosed as emotionally disturbed. They are at greater risk for schizophrenia, autism, sexual addiction, alcoholism, bed wetting, and all forms of antisocial and criminal behavior."[19] And every study I've ever seen regarding young criminals points to boys with no real dad and young men who hate their father.

Let me suggest two things. First, the identity we seek in the work force robs us of time and energy, thwarting engagement with our families, specifically our sons. Second, our lack of contribution to family values (as well as church, school, and community values) degrades the resilience against cultural decay. Our boys are absorbing the brunt of this decay. Without a change in this trend, our legacy as men will prove to be very unimpressive – unless, of course, the "love of money" reflects well on us. But that doesn't bear out according to a well-known bible verse (1 Timothy 6:10).

According to a *Focus on the Family Magazine* ad for *Bringing Up Boys Videos*, "For healthier boys, parents must understand the power and influence of fathers and other adult male role models."[20] I agree. Dads must step up to the plate. It's imperative that men team together as we mentor our boys. And we must also reach out to the boys who are growing up without a significant, positive, male role model.

PROMISE KEEPERS 2000

I listened to Josh McDowell speak in Dallas at the 2000 Promise Keepers event. The man is a powerful speaker. What passion. And what a testimony. I learned a simple phrase from that talk. That phrase packs so much wisdom in just six words. I have alluded to it several times already. And here it is: "Rules without relationship lead to rebellion."

The idea goes like this (and I'll let Dr. Dobson do the talking again): "The essence of my message is that you as parents must work harder than ever at building satisfying and affirming relationships with your kids. You must give them a desire to stay within the confines of the family and conform to its systems of beliefs. ... It still makes sense to prohibit harmful or immoral behavior, but those prohibitions must be supplemented by an emotional closeness that makes children want to do what is right. ... Author and speaker Josh McDowell expressed this principle in a single sentence. He said, 'Rules without relationship lead to rebellion.'"[21]

Here's how I apply this inspiring insight. When I recognize a hint of rebellion in one of my kids, I attack the problem on two fronts. First, I repeat, *first*, I evaluate my current relationship with him or her. My relationship with my child can have peaks and valleys within a single day. I am the adult in the relationship and I am the one responsible for nurturing it. I ask myself, "What can I do to enhance or develop a stronger relationship?" Or even more important, "What have I neglected, letting the relationship slip?"

After I have taken steps to mend any relationship issues, I *then* teach truth, *biblical truth*, as it applies to my parental authority and established rules. I wish I could pull this off without bringing into it personal pride and frustration, but often I can't. My wife and I significantly improve our success at this by helping and encouraging each other.

Also remember, Jesus is the source of our strength. And the glory of Jesus is "full of grace and truth" (John 1:14). I read an internet commentary on that verse that summed it up with simplicity and wisdom: "Truth shines; grace is given." If I can let *truth shine* by itself and keep my lectures to an absolute minimum, and *give grace*, even in the midst of fatherly discipline, I become more aligned with Jesus' example of relationship and authority.

Now, absorb this bit of wisdom: "By the time you realize your father was right, you've got a son who thinks you are wrong." What does this say of dads' presentation of *truth*? Let me state it bluntly. Cramming truth down our children's throat rather than letting truth shine, while neglecting to give *grace,* results in this father/son relationship anomaly. Think about it.

Dr. Dobson offers this for those with younger children: "...the day is coming when those of you with young children will need to draw on the foundation of love and caring that you have built. If resentment and rejection characterized the early years, the adolescent experience might be a nightmare. The best way to avoid this teenage time bomb is to defuse it in childhood. That is done with a healthy balance of authority and love at home. Begin now to build a relationship that will see you through the storms of adolescence."[22]

50/50?

Armed with an understanding of parental relationship and authority, I envisioned a 50/50 balance. I would maintain 50% relationship and 50% authority. 60/40 would put me out of balance and rebellion or disrespect would be my kids' natural response. But the more I thought about this 50/50 balance, I realized it put me at only half friend and half authority to my kids. Something didn't seem right about that.

I then reassessed my view. I should be 100% friend and 100% authority to my kids. This was still a balanced approach. If my kids began to rebel, I would probably discover I had fallen to 75/100, 75% friend and 100% authority. Rather than balancing 75/75 by backing off as authority, I would bring my relationship back up to 100%, finding the appropriate balance back at 100/100. Likewise, if my kids began treating me like a peer, not respecting my authority, I would reestablish authority back to 100%.

But one can overdo it. I recognized that 110% friendship established a buddy/buddy relationship, putting me at an inappropriate peer level with them. Conversely, 110% authority resulted in an overly authoritarian relationship, beating them down with discipline, correction and lecture. The Bible says, "Fathers, do not exasperate your children; instead, bring them up in the training and instruction of the Lord." (Ephesians 6:4) and "Fathers, do not embitter your children, or they will become discouraged" (Colossians 3:21).

As your kids get older and begin phasing into a more independent lifestyle (maybe thirteen to fifteen years old), they will begin to prefer the company of their friends over family. We all know this to be quite normal, although this shouldn't happen too early. An attempt to maintain 100% friendship will likely smother them. Hanging on to the 100% authority status will not help prepare them for a responsible and independent life. So the time comes when you begin to phase out. You prepare to release them. You can imagine a balanced approach would look something like 80% relationship, 80% authority. Then 60/60. By the time your young adult goes off to college or other higher learning (in other words, out of the house but still a dependent on your tax return) you may be at 25/25. You are still a friend and you still maintain some authority status.

Having said all that, I have discovered that a slight variation to this approach may be required. This applies especially to fathers with sons. As you approach the big release (you've probably heard the "releasing the kite" story) you may find it necessary to back off on the authority role. Your son may really want the independence - I mean *really* want it. As much you may want to control him or even think you can control him, you can't. If he resists and or rebels, by all means, maintain the relationship. Do not insist on maintaining hard and fast rules at the expense of your relationship with him.

Dr. Kevin Leman has an appropriate phrase that is a variation from Josh McDowell's, "We don't parent by rules; we parent teenagers by relationship." He later states:

> When it comes to raising adolescents, "rules" become outdated almost as soon as they become relevant. Parenting teens is an ongoing, fluid process. Kids in this stage grow up so fast that parenting teens needs to become far more about building relationships than about living by hard-and-fast rules.[23]

I recommended earlier that you read at least six books about raising teenagers. One I recommend is Joe White's *Sticking With Your Teen*. Here's an excerpt that reinforces the above statements.

> A lot of parents, especially Christian ones, try the "crackdown." Determined to make their teens submit to authority, they haul out the howitzers – rules on stone tablets, year-long groundings, sermonettes, house arrest.
>
> The problem is that these parents don't realize their job description has changed since their kids were little. Teens need parents who have moved from governor to mentor, from commander to coach, from benevolent dictator to guide. It's time to be an advisor, not a puppet master.
>
> The trick, I learned, is allowing the transition to happen gradually. Start off firm, slowly giving way to more liberty. If you come in with handcuffs, you'll become a controlling, frustrated parent with a rebellious teen.

The truth is that our kids need us more than ever when they're teens. Not as controllers, but as counselors.[24]

The best phase of raising a teen may be the last phase. I can't speak from experience yet, but when he's finally on his own, you become 100% friend again and you drop the authority status altogether. Then you patiently wait for the day the grandkids come into the picture. Finally, you spoil those little rascals as a means of payback (Be nice, you're actually supposed to reinforce what your kids, the new parents, are teaching). And the cycle starts all over again as your kids attempt the same balanced approach with their children.

Rules without relationship lead to rebellion.

Truth shines; grace is given.

BIBLICAL FATHERHOOD

God's word offers much on fatherhood. Not to exclude raising daughters, but let's look to scripture for guidance on mentoring our boys.

You shall love the Lord your God with all your heart and with all your soul and with all your might. These words, which I am commanding you today, shall be on your heart. You shall teach them diligently to your sons and talk of them when you sit in your house and when you walk by the way and when you lie down and when you rise up. (Deuteronomy 6:5-7, NASB)

Dave Simmons expands on this in *Dad the Family Mentor*: "The word *diligence* means to sharpen, to assail, to wound, or to pierce with enthusiasm. You must shape and fashion the teaching in such a way that it has enough puncture power to spear the heart. ... 'Teach with diligence' also means to keep teaching consistently, without ever giving up. *Diligence* means to practice regularly or to teach daily."[25]

We see a most wonderful model of father/son mentoring from King Solomon to his son in the book of Proverbs. He wrote the book to his son "for attaining wisdom and discipline..." (Proverbs 1:2). He repeatedly implores, "Listen, my son, to your father's instruction and do not forsake your mother's teaching" (Proverbs 1:8). Solomon sums it up: "The glory of sons is their fathers" (Proverbs 17:6, NASB).

Dads, there's a war going on. And the biggest battle in this war is between you and the culture. It's your masculine leadership in opposition to Satan's evil. It's your fatherhood verses peer influence. You must prevail.

Chapter 3

From Role Model to Mentor

Ionce introduced a *Bringing Up Boys* teaching topic by
quoting from the book's author, Dr. James Dobson. *He*
had masterfully built on his teaching point with a clear and
logical explanation. But *I* went straight to *his* punch line:
"Elementary classrooms ... are designed primarily by
women to fit the temperament and learning styles of girls."[1]
Now, because I had studied several resources supporting this
idea, in my mind it made intuitive sense; or so I thought. In
fact, I declared the point with a hint of humor, trying to set
the tone for the rest of the class period. Boy did I set the tone;
but not as I had intended.

A few more minutes into the class a gentleman inter-
rupted, "Excuse me, Jeff, I think you have a few ladies
sitting back here squirming in their seats. I think they're
school teachers."

I immediately felt a warm sensation flush through my
whole body. "Open mouth, insert foot," I thought. How am I
going to recover from this?

The first words out of my mouth were, "Dobson said it!
He explains it well." Now would you believe I had an oppor-
tunity to tell this story to Dr. Dobson recently? He responded,
"Oh sure, blame it on me." But it gets worse. The next words

out of my mouth to the school teachers were, "actually we homeschool."

Oops, not a good answer. Not only had I dug myself into a hole, I was burying myself in it! There was no recovering now.

The following week, class attendance dropped a bit. Only those returning got the benefit of a better-prepared explanation of Dr. Dobson's point. Two lessons *re*learned: First, know your audience; second, it's all in the delivery.

So here's the explanation. And we'll see the significance of this explanation as we discover: *masculinity is bestowed by masculinity.*

BRINGING UP BOYS, CHAPTER 13: BOYS IN SCHOOL

Simply put:

Almost every authority on child development recognizes that schools are typically not set up to accommodate the unique needs of boys. Elementary classrooms, especially, are designed primarily by women to fit the temperament and learning styles of girls.[2]

John Eldredge sees the dilemma as well: "The average schoolteacher faces an incredible challenge: to bring order to a room of boys and girls, and promote learning. The main obstacle to that noble goal is getting the boys to sit still, keep quiet, and pay attention ... for an entire day. You might as well hold back the tide. That's not the way a boy is wired, and it's not the way a boy learns. Rather than changing the way we do male education, we try to change males."[3]

J. Richard Fugate takes this concern a step further. "Most men in the 21st century have been raised mostly by female caregivers."[4] Think about it – from grade school teachers to Sunday School teachers, from day-caregivers to soccer moms. Even the Boy Scouts welcome female adult Scout Masters – the women go camping with the boys. Dr. Dobson shares this from his research: Sociologist Peter Karl believes that because boys spend up to 80 percent of their time with women, they don't know how to act as men when they grow up.[5]

And to boot, it is only natural for moms to resist their son's innate desire to one day detach from her. While dad becomes "all that" when the lad turns about age three to five, moms continue to crave lots of hugs and kisses, quiet story times, and gentle tickle games. Moms are discouraged by grass stains on the knees, knots on the head, and dirt where dirt shouldn't get. All the while, these moms may not be aware of the masculine identity trying to emerge. Her young man is trying to "formulate a masculine identity."[6] She does not understand that she is, according to Dr. Dobson, "… in his way. If she is too close, the child may feel swallowed up by her. After all, she is a woman. She stands between him and being a man."[7]

Don't get me wrong. The young man will need to learn how to relate with femininity. Mom can help him by teaching him to treat her like a lady, with love and honor. But Dad (and/ or other men) should become his primary teacher/mentor.

MASCULINITY IS *BESTOWED*

John Eldridge, in *Wild at Heart*, sums it up:

Masculinity is *bestowed*. A boy learns who he is and what he's got from a man, or the company of men. He cannot learn it any other place. He cannot learn it from other boys, and he cannot learn it from the world of women. The plan from the beginning of

59

time was that his father would lay the foundation for a young boy's heart, and pass on to him that essential knowledge and confidence in his strength.[8]

It's a simple and basic concept. The best football coaches are football players. The most qualified math teachers are mathematicians. For manhood mentoring – boys need *men*!

The converse of this idea – need I say it? Let's go to the experts again. Gary Smalley and John Trent put it like this, "… the logical conclusion of excluding our sons from our lives is that they pick up a feminized version of masculinity from Mom or a distorted image of manhood from peers."[9] And James Dobson offers a quote that, taken out of context, would get me in trouble again. "The truth is, Dad is more important than Mom." You see, put in *proper* context, we find Dr. Dobson says, "In my opinion (and in the opinion of an increasing number of researchers), the father plays an essential role in a boy's normal development as a man." He concludes, "Mothers make boys. Fathers make men."[10] I say … actually, I've gotten into enough trouble; I think I'll defer my comment.

But what does this mean for boys of single moms? The answer to that question is revealed in a story from Brian Molitor's *Boy's Passage – Man's Journey.* While illustrating rites of passage ceremonies from cultures of the past, he tells of a boy named White Fox. This young lad was a member of the Lakota tribe from a territory that is now called South Dakota. He had lost his father to battle wounds from an attacking band of renegades.

Throughout the years his father's friends had treated him as their own son. Early on these loving mentors showed White Fox how to ride the painted ponies that seemed to fly across the grasslands. He remembered the time one of the elders presented him with his first bow and a quiver of hand-painted arrows. Fondly he recalled the many evenings spent sitting silently near the watering holes with these quiet warriors, waiting for mule deer to appear. As they talked together, these men taught him about the ways of a warrior. They took time to teach him about the changes that he would experience on his journey to manhood. From these times of training, White Fox learned about the importance of a man's honor and the responsibilities of community leadership.[11]

And these Native Americans may have known nothing of God's heart for these fatherless boys. For He is "A father to the fatherless" (Psalm 68:5).

While you, the readers, are pursuing a plan for mentoring your own sons, I will be interjecting this idea of reaching out to the fatherless. Let's just say I have an ulterior motive – to recruit mentors for the fatherless boys, boys under *your* circle of influence. They need you. Their moms are desperate for a mentor for their sons – a mentor like *you*.

THE ROLE MODEL

Now there's a buzzword: *role model*. Let's look to the NBA. From David Robinson to Dennis Rodman, our boys are influenced by role models – some good ones, some bad. Of course, some, like Charles Barkley, refuse to accept the responsibility of being a role model. But, nonetheless, kids look up to a certain kind of person. They want to "be like Mike." And that's the key. Kids want to mimic the behavior of their role models.

So how do we define role model? Webster says: a person whose behavior in a particular role is imitated by others.[12] By all means a suitable definition, however, this is a modern on-line definition. Now let's go to Noah Webster's definition

61

of model from 1828. Pertaining to a model, as in a person to be imitated: "A pattern; any thing to be imitated. Take Cicero, lord Chatham or Burke, as a model of eloquence; take Washington as a model of prudence, integrity and patriotism; above all, let Christ be the model of our benevolence, humility, obedience and patience."[13] Couldn't have said it better myself.

The bottom line, we look to role models to set a *good* example. Whether a professional athlete, movie star, rock star, the President of the United States, or Dad, a good role model will help our kids as they grow. A bad one, on the other hand, will also help them grow – in the wrong direction.

Notice, Dad, you're on the list. You are a role model, even if you, like Charles Barkley, don't want to accept that responsibility. Dave Simmons writes in *Dad the Family Mentor*, "The good news – your children will copy you. The bad news – your children will copy you." "Children are natural mimics; they act like their parents... So you'd better make sure they have something worthwhile to copy."[14]

Some of this mimicked behavior is done subconsciously. Your sons may copy your technique for turning the steering wheel; hand over hand, one finger inside the wheel, or, if you're really cool, one-handed open palm on the wheel. If you leave the toilet seat up, you can bet your son will. And chances are, *your* dad did also.

Some of the mimicked behavior is by conscious choice. If you've always owned Fords, your son may prefer them as well. And again, we can go to generations past to find the source of this pattern.

Some mimicked behavior has significant effects on our son's lives and the lives of many others. He may follow your footsteps in his career choice. If you are a parametric cost-analyst, predicting the cost of technologies that don't even exist yet, he may think that's pretty cool, just because that's what Dad does (you geek!). One young boy I know by the name of Greg couldn't decide whether to be an NBA basketball player or a gourmet chef. What would make a kid be torn between two totally different careers? He loved basketball; his dad was a chef.

Robert Lewis shares this story in *Raising a Modern-Day Knight*:

> On a snowy day, General Robert E. Lee took his eight-year-old son, Custis, out for a walk. Wearied by the high drifts, Custis began to fall behind his father.
>
> After a few minutes Lee looked back and found that his boy was behind him, imitating his every move and walking in the tracks the father had made in the snow. "When I saw this," Lee told one of his friends long afterwards, "I said to myself, it behooves me to walk very straight when this fellow is already following in my tracks."[15]

Scripture has some wonderful words on modeling. Titus 2:6-7 first implores men to "encourage the young men to be self-controlled." Paul then suggests a basic principle for modeling: "In everything set them an example by doing what is good." Yes! *Set them an example!* And if they are going to mimic your example, you better be *"doing what is good."*

JESUS AS A ROLE MODEL

Following the Last Supper, we see that Jesus modeled for his disciples by setting an example. In the book of John, verse 13:5:

After that, he poured water into a basin and began to wash his disciples' feet, drying them with the towel that was wrapped around him.

Jesus didn't explain what he was up to. He just set the example for them to follow. Without an explanation, Peter was uncomfortable about his Lord serving him in such a way. Peter resisted because he didn't understand.

So the Teacher explained his actions. John 13:14-15:

Now that I, your Lord and Teacher, have washed your feet, you also should wash one another's feet. I have *set an example* that you should do as I have done for you. (italics mine)

O.K. Peter, you can't argue with that.

JESUS' ROLE MODEL

I tell you the truth, the Son can do nothing by himself; he can do only what he sees his Father doing, because whatever the Father does the Son also does. (John 5:19)

Wouldn't we all love for our teenage sons to have that attitude? They sure did when they were younger. They copied our every move. But as our sons get older, they realize we are not perfect like God the Father. So hopefully (and prayerfully) they saw Jesus in us when they were young and then as teenagers look to their Savior as their Role Model.

WHAT'S ON YOUR MIND?

We know your son learns from what he observes. But if he learns only what you model, his lessons are limited to your modeled *actions*. He cannot effectively apply these lessons to other circumstances unless he knows *why* you take certain actions.

Robert Lewis' story tells of an abusive father. His is not a testimony of a positive role model, but Dr. Lewis' story illustrates an important lesson.

I never knew what he believed. His inner world was a mystery to me. We never sat together and talked about life or girls or sex or school or the future. There was no fatherly preparation for things ahead.[16]

Does your son know what's on your mind? If what he sees, he does, can he see your thought life? The part of your life you'd like most for your son to mimic involves your thought life, your decisions and choices. (Or maybe you don't want them to.) This requires *more* than modeling.

MENTORING – A GREAT LEAD-IN BY DR. DOBSON:

My point through this discussion has been to urge those of you who are young fathers to provide that modeling on which your boys can build their masculine identities. ...your sons will observe who you are and thereby learn to serve in a similar way when they are grown.

If modeling is the first, *the second deals with the specific instruction that dads should transmit to their sons.* That subject could fill many books... [like this one]

In short, this kind of specific instruction is the substance of your responsibility to affirm, recognize, and celebrate your son's journey into manhood.

Chief among our concerns is the absence of masculine role modeling and *mentoring* that dads should be providing.[17] (*italics mine*)

65

Yes, Dr. Dobson. Where modeling is certainly important and significant, it is mentoring that is exponentially effective: teaching, showing and explaining.

While Scripture enlightened us with words on modeling, we can go to those very same verses to find God's plan for mentoring.

JESUS' MENTOR

We know Jesus looked to His Father as his model. Remember from just a few pages ago? "I tell you the truth, the Son can do nothing by himself; he can do only what he sees his Father doing, because whatever the Father does the Son also does" (John 5:19). Now let's go to the very next verse:

> For the Father loves the Son and *shows* him all he does. Yes, to your amazement he will *show* him even greater things than these. (*italics mine*)

This "like-Father-like-Son" rapport went beyond a mere role-model relationship. Out of love, the Father *showed* Him. Perhaps He explained, illustrated, and demonstrated for His Son.

JESUS AS A MENTOR

We found that God's Word illustrates the role-model relationship between Jesus and His disciples. After washing their feet, He said, "I have set you an example that you should do as I have done for you" (John 13:15). But as we discovered, setting the example without an explanation actually confused those who observed. So we continue with the story in John 13 to find Jesus the Mentor expanded His modeling with the appropriate teaching:

I tell you the truth, no servant is greater than his master, nor is a messenger greater than the one who sent him. Now that you know these things, you will be blessed if you do them. (vs. 16-17)

TITUS 2 MENTORING

The passages on teaching found in the Book of Titus chapter 2 have inspired many. Some have even organized ministries under the "Titus 2" name. We discovered earlier from a passage here that men are to model for the young men by "setting them an example by doing what is good." And as we have also discovered the need to expand on our modeling, we find in verse 8:

In your *teaching* show integrity, seriousness and soundness of speech that cannot be condemned. (italics mine)

We are to *teach*. We are to *explain*. We are to *show*. We are to *mentor*.

MORE FROM THE BIBLE ON TEACHING

You then, my son, be strong in the grace that is in Christ Jesus. And the things you have heard me say in the presence of many witnesses entrust to reliable men who will also be qualified to teach others (2 Timothy 2:1-2).

And the Lord's servant must not quarrel; instead, he must be kind to everyone, able to teach, not resentful. Those who oppose him he must gently instruct, in the hope that God will grant them repentance leading them to a knowledge of the truth, ... (2 Timothy 2:24-25).

Teach the older men to be temperate, worthy of respect, self-controlled, and sound in faith, in love and in endurance (Titus 2:2).

Not many of you should presume to be teachers, my brothers, because you know that we who teach will be judged more strictly (James 3:1).

FROM ROLE MODEL TO MENTOR

With our emphasis on teaching, showing, explaining – how do we mentor a nine month old baby or a two year old toddler? How do we teach financial wisdom to a seven year old or translate "love your wife as Christ loved the church" to a ten year old. Obviously we must take into account the young protégé's communication skills and his maturity to comprehend as we transition from *role model* to *mentor*.

In the early years, our kids will have no ability to verbally communicate. They learn from what they put their eyes on, put their hands on, and to our dismay, put their tongues on. They have a natural curiosity to see, feel and taste. Even if they have discovered for the first time the brown blob left in the grass by the dog – first they see it, then they touch it, and if we don't get to them first, then they taste it. During this stage of life we *model*.

It's important to be aware of the things your kids are learning at this point. Because verbal expression is a small part of our overall communication, two key issues for this learning stage include facial expressions and body language. Your kids are learning appropriate facial expressions and body language by observation. I can always tell if parents smile a lot by initiating a smile to their baby and observing his response. Smiling parents have smiling babies. But if you scowl a lot, your kids will scowl a lot. If you put your elbows on the table, your kids will.

You must fully understand the significance of your job as a *role model* during this period. If you put the toilet lid down, your son will.

As your kids get older they will learn to communicate verbally. With their evolving mastery of the tongue, they will continue to observe you, your choice of words and your tone of voice. They will mimic you every step of the way. So you're still *modeling*. But now you can bring into your fatherhood repertoire a hint of teaching. I warn you, however, don't set an early precedence by giving full explanations for every teaching and disciplining moment. Instead, teach your kids at an early age of God's creation, His love, and of the job He gave you and your wife as parents. Help your kids understand you are their friend and their authority. Expect obedience according to this definition: immediate, complete, correct, without complaint and without challenge. Only when your kids respond to your authority with proper obedience should you begin to offer teaching explanations.

By the time your kids are teenagers, they will need much more explanation. They should still honor your parental authority, but you should honor them with appropriate explanation. This will help them as they take ownership of the truths you have been teaching all along.

As your kids transition from simple observation to a desire to understand, you will transition from *role model* to *mentor*. But one final point to make with this – *mentoring always incorporates modeling*.

WHAT MAKES A MENTOR?

Unlike the role model, a mentor cannot operate from the TV or movie screen, from a stage or from a ball field or court. Although the role model does influence kids from these places of work, he does not interact with his audience. The mentor must interact with his protégé to carry out his charge. And for dads, it's just as Sam Mehaffie points out: "Just being in the home is not good enough; dads must take an active role in their boys' lives."[18]

Two basic conditions establish a mentorship position. The first entails *appointment* to a position involving mentorship interaction. The second involves *earned* relationship, respect, credibility and accountability. While either or both are necessary, a person in an *appointed* position can fall short of influencing his apprentice by failing to *earn* a relationship.

Examples of *appointed* mentors include coach, schoolteacher, Scoutmaster, Sunday School teacher and, yes, you the parent are appointed by God as mentor of your children. It is important for you to also understand that every appointed mentor is operating under delegated authority. The authority of your son's schoolteacher is delegated by you the parent. Even the authority for you to raise your own kids is delegated by the Creator.

Establishment of the *earned* mentorship position has many facets. From positive to negative, obvious to insidious, requested to unsolicited. A person can develop a mentorship relationship with or without the appointed title. He can also initiate influence on your kids without your awareness.

I can't remember where I read or heard this story, but it illustrates the possibilities for a mentor to earn or create a mentorship relationship with an impressionable youngster. The story goes like this: A man spends some time in his driveway shoot'n hoops. A teenage boy happens to walk by. They neither speak nor even make eye contact. On another day, the boy walks by and meets eyes with the man. The man greets him and gets a shy "hey" from the boy. On still another day, the boy walks by the man's driveway game. This time the man says, "Hey, how's it go'in?" The boy offers a response, losing some of the shyness from the previous day. As this continues, the man eventually convinces the boy to shoot hoops with him. Over several games of H-O-R-S-E and Around-the-World, they begin talking. First, small talk, but as the boy becomes more comfortable, he lets his guard down. The man is able to get into the boy's life, offering advice and council. He earns the boy's respect. The man is eventually able to offer accountability to this young man. You can see the possibilities here. Does the man have good or bad motives? Is the boy even aware of the dynamics of this new friendship? Do the boy's parents know of this relationship, and if they do, do they approve of it?

Notice the *relationship/authority* facets in each version of the mentor/protégé process. We see the same balance required for proper parenting. The appointed mentor starts with the positional *authority* and must develop a *relationship*. The earned mentorship position starts with a *relationship* then typically progresses to a position of respect and *authority*.

A PLAN

I've heard this phrase before, but I'm going to give Brian Molitor credit for his quote in *Boy's Passage – Man's Journey*: "If you don't care where you are going, any road will get you there." Another one he offers: "If you fail to plan, you plan to fail." Mr. Molitor goes on to say, "In other words, if you really don't have a destination in mind, it is never clear when you are going in the right – or wrong – direction."[19] Robert Lewis points out that fathers lack a *directional process* that calls their sons to embrace the manhood they should be able to define. I think we often don't know where we should be taking our boys in their manhood journey. Or we may know where we want to go but don't know how to get there. The bottom line: we must have a comprehensive plan; a plan we can stick with.

"The plans of a man's heart are like deep water. A man of understanding draws them out" (Proverbs 20:5, NASB). I was that man once; the man with plans in my heart that wouldn't surface. But eventually they were drawn out and I discovered a plan that works.

Here are some elements of a plan I think we can all stick with. (Sorry, bad grammar. "...with which we can stick" just didn't sound right.) They are employed in the context of a formalized group. First, invite a few others to join you and make a roster of names. Then establish a group name – something cool and inspiring. Establish a routine schedule for meeting together. Select a location or a rotation of places to meet. Pick a leader or at least a primary facilitator. Brainstorm activities the guys may want to participate in together. Finally, pursue a lesson and discussion plan with a Christ-centered manhood theme.

This group format may have some familiarity to it. You may already be involved in a group-mentoring program called football or basketball, or Boys Scouts, or even Sunday School. The only missing mentorship element in these groups may be the Christ-centered "manhood training." In chapter 5, I'll take you step by step through the group plan and expand on every detail of this process. I'll even explain how to implement manhood training into Sunday school, Boy Scouts, team sports or even after-school programs at public schools.

Each of these elements of your plan may be critical, but the primary vision centers on the teaching. Therefore, your plan must include superb manhood training themes. Dr. Lewis refers to a "well defined set of ideals." Numerous curriculums are available as well as many other types of teaching resources, but a well-defined set of ideals will give you and your boys a common reference throughout the mentoring process. While chapter 5 will touch on this, my son and I will also offer an expanded explanation of our set of ideals in a co-written follow-on book. Look for it in the near future on www.SquiresToKnights.com. You can also find free resources for this effort on www.Squires2Knights. com.

Dr. Lewis continues, "As a symbol of manhood, a knight's chivalry points to one of the most pressing needs of young men in our generation: a well-defined set of ideals. Ideals set parameters; they shape a boy's identity and motivate him to higher levels of excellence, ..."[20] If each of you memorize your set of ideals, spontaneous teaching opportunities are more easily capitalized.

An example of this concept is illustrated in a group discussion I once led. I asked the boys to answer the question: What does it mean to be a man? As each boy shared a perspective on the question, I was able to relate his comment to one of twelve memorized character themes. These character themes have defined the teaching topics for each of our monthly meetings for almost five years. They have given us a common language, helping us communicate ideas and vision. After over an hour of responses to the question, we had hit each of our twelve themes at least once. I concluded our discussion by highlighting the comprehensive nature of our twelve manhood themes based on their answers to the original question. Because of our familiarity with our "well defined set of ideals," this entire discussion was done spontaneously and without notes.

The final element necessary for your success with group mentoring entails *commitment*. Commitment is the principal reason I believe mentoring in the context of a group is paramount. Within a group, you have built-in accountability. Just as a workout partner keeps you from sleeping in and skipping your 5:00 a.m. workout commitment (the phone will ring at 5:05 if you're not at the gym), fellow group members can help you stick with your plan. In addition, loyalty increases when you know there is a group counting on you.

From *Seven Promises of a Promise Keeper*: "We need like-minded friends. We need support, encouragement, and maybe even an occasional boot in the rear to help us keep that and the other commitments called for in this book." The author is introducing "Promise 2: A Man and His Mentors." He goes on to say, "The concept of those who are more mature helping those who are less mature is called *mentoring*."[21]

Dennis Rainey offers five steps to manhood. Step number four is called MENTOR. He says, "I believe God has more for men beyond manhood; I believe He wants us to become *mentors* to other men. As He teaches us, we reach out with His wisdom and love to boys who are facing adolescence, to teens who need to move to manhood, and to the men who need to become mentors. *Every man ought to make it his goal to be a mentor to someone.*"[22]

About a third of the men who have participated in our small group do not have a son in the group. My father joins us, giving us the perspective of a patriarch. My brother Clark, a father of only daughters, joins us as one of my best friends. (Just before I sent this manuscript in for printing, Clark was blessed with a son.) Another best friend began with the mentoring group by sponsoring a boy who lost his father to cancer. Several are step-dads to the boys they accompany. Finally, several men have commented to me about the growth *they* have experienced while participating in our mentoring effort. The blessings abound.

I close with the lyrics of one of my favorite songs. *Phillips, Craig and Dean* sings *I Want to Be Just Like You*. The chorus goes like this:

I want to be just like you,
Cause he wants to be just like me.
I want to be a holy example   [role model]
For his innocent eyes to see.
Help me be a living Bible, Lord,
For my little boy to read.   [mentor]
I want to be just like you,
Cause he wants to be just like me.[23]

Chapter 4

Mentoring Priorities

I would like to address a question that has been asked over and over and over – and over again. We all know the answer – consider it a rhetorical question.

At the end of your life, when you look back, are you going to wish you had spent more time at work, made more money, or bought more stuff?

The classic, melodramatic illustration of the answer to this great question is often portrayed through the lyrics of Harry Chapin's *Cats in the Cradle*. You know, "…there were planes to catch, and bills to pay."

And like any boy, the son asks: "When you coming home, dad?"

Answer: "I don't know when, but we'll get together then. You know we'll have a good time then."

But where does the time go: "…it occurred to me, he'd grown up just like me. My boy was just like me."[1]

This is the opposite cry from that of *Phillips, Craig, and Dean,* as I quoted their lyrics at the close of the last chapter.

BIBLICAL PERSPECTIVES

When teaching basic Christian values, we often hear the same popular scripture verses to make certain points. Case in point: "Money is the root of all evil" (1 Timothy 6:10, NASB). Even the secular world likes to quote that verse, probably often unaware that it comes from the Christian Bible. By the way, did you catch the missing word in the scripture quote? It's the *"love* of money" that is the root of all evil.

The point I'm trying to make here centers on priorities. If we are to go from role model to mentor, we must first model proper Biblical priorities. Then we must teach from those priorities.

So let's first put our lives in the proper perspective – a Biblical perspective. Then we'll relate our discoveries with the mentoring of our boys.

CAREERISM:

Let's first consider our employment. If we were to jot down a list of pros and cons concerning our commitment to work, what would it look like?

PROS	CONS
A noble cause	Busy
Provision	Desire for more (greed)
Income	Lack of time with wife
Material possessions	Lack of time with kids
Job satisfaction	Lack of masculine influence
Identity	on sons

What if we made a similar list for a different plan, putting family ahead of work?

PROS	CONS
Busyness kept in check	Less income
Reduced materialism	Less stuff
Appreciation for what we do have	
Time for wife	
Time for kids	
Emphasis on family unity	

Our friend, Dr. Dobson, points out that "America's materialistic value system runs very deep within our culture." He wasn't saying that in a complimentary way. However, he also points out "...middle-income couples ... [were] scaling back ... for the sake of the children. They were taking more time off and, when necessary, they were lowering their standard of living to accommodate the loss of income."[2]

The Bible proclaims:

A good name is more desirable than great riches... (Proverbs 22:1).

Then Jesus said to his disciples, "I tell you the truth, it is hard for a rich man to enter the kingdom of heaven (Matthew 19:23).

The brother in humble circumstances ought to take pride in his high position. But the one who is rich should take pride in his low position, because he will pass away like a wild flower (James 1:9-10).

You have lived on earth in luxury and self-indulgence. You have fattened yourselves in the day of slaughter (James 5:5).

The other perspective the Bible offers to our discussion:

He who finds a wife finds what is good and receives favor from the Lord (Proverbs 18:22).

Sons are a heritage from the Lord,
    children a reward from him.
Like arrows in the hands of a warrior
    are sons born in one's youth.
Blessed is the man
    whose quiver is full of them (Psalm 127:3-5).

Point made!

Let's do that again! This time our list will consider the pros and cons of being a good husband. We will then compare that list to a similar one considering a failed marriage (with or without divorce).

GOOD HUSBAND:

PROS	CONS
God's design	NONE
Love	
Support	
Needs met	
Double my retirement	
(divorce splits retirement	
fund in half)	

FAILED MARRIAGE:

PROS	CONS
~~Can bail out when times get tough~~ (It's what we all probably did when playing the dating game as teens.) Scratch that. NONE	Outside God's design Bitterness Loss of spousal support Low self-esteem Abuse Emptiness

Notice the two apposing quadrants are either full or empty. Sure makes it easy for a guy to make a decision. So why so many divorces? That's for another book by a different author.

The Bible, of course, has a few things to say about this:

The Lord God said, "It is not good for the man to be alone. I will make a helper suitable for him" (Genesis 2:18).

May your fountain be blessed, and may you rejoice in the wife of your youth (Proverbs 5:18).

Husbands, love your wives, just as Christ loved the church and gave himself up for her to make her holy, ... (Ephesians 5:25).

In the same way, you husbands must give honor to your wives. Treat her with understanding as you live together. She may be weaker than you are, but she is your equal partner in God's gift of new life. If you don't treat her as you should, your prayers will not be heard (1 Peter 3:7, NASB).

"Haven't you read," he replied, "that at the beginning the Creator 'made them male and female,' and said, 'For this reason a man shall leave his father and mother and be united to his wife, and the two will become one flesh'? So they are no longer two, but one. Therefore what God has joined together, *let man not separate*" (Matthew 19:4-6, *italics mine*).

Nuff said!
We could continue.
Fatherhood compared to poor or no relationship with your children:

FATHERHOOD:

PROS	CONS
God's design	NONE
Love	
Teaching/training	
Sense of security for kids	
Healthy masculinity for boy	

Poor or no relationship with kids:

PROS	CONS
NONE	Outside God's design No male influence for kids Or poor male influence for kids Abuse For kids – increased possibility of Low self-esteem Low grades Drug abuse Sexual activity Criminal acts Violence

Remember some of the conclusions made by studies referenced in Chapter 2? We found the absence of the father's influence was very destructive for the children. Many want to convince themselves that kids are resilient and will recover and heal from the pain of the family breakup. It just doesn't happen that way.

The Word says:

> For I have chosen him, so that he will direct his children and his household after him to keep the way of the Lord by doing what is right and just, so that the Lord will bring about for Abraham what he has promised him (Genesis 18:19).

> Love the Lord your God with all your heart and with all your soul and with all your strength. These commandments that I give you today are to be upon

your hearts. Impress them on your children. Talk about them when you sit at home and when you walk along the road, when you lie down and when you get up (Deuteronomy 6:5-7).

The glory of sons is their fathers (Proverbs 17:6, NASB).

Fathers, do not embitter your children, or they will become discouraged (Colossians 3:21).

He must manage his own family well and see that his children obey him with proper respect. (If anyone does not know how to manage his own family, how can he take care of God's church?) (1 Timothy 3:4-5).

A final note that paints a grim picture of today's reality for marriage and fatherhood – with divorce rates at 50% or more, a study showed that three years after divorce, less than half the men ever see their kids again ... *ever!* That hurts – that hurts real bad, guys. An additional bit of data indicates that last year (2006) 36.8% of births were to unmarried women.[3] What does all this say about the future of the husband and father roles? Here's an example: from a TV interview with a celebrity – "I was with that chick for six years [not married] – got two little boys out of it - ... oh, it didn't work out..."

Unfortunately, there are a growing number of men who have desperately tried to save their marriages only to have their wives give up on them. The divorce goes through and custody issues abound. Some of these men become single dads, while others, probably most, battle for every hour of time with their kids. These men need encouragement; they need support. Team mentorship programs can be invaluable resources for them.

Our last pro/con list – Disciple of God vs. follower of culture (no faith, once a week or maybe only twice a year church attendance, little or no walk with the Lord):

DISCIPLE OF GOD:

PROS	CONS
Salvation Eternal Life Holy Spirit Blessing Sanctification Hope Fruits of the Spirit Gifting Good Works	NONE

FOLLOWER OF CULTURE:

PROS	CONS
NONE	Disconnected from God Hell Self-centeredness Self-sufficiency No Hope Emptiness

Dr. Ray Vanderlaun, otherwise known as RVL, is an incredible Bible teacher. He makes scripture come alive by relating evidence of the ancient Jewish culture. In the title of his ministry, *In the Dust of the Messiah*, RVL portrays a wonderful image of the disciples of the day. He explains that a disciple would pursue his mentor's tutelage with such vigor, following his master so closely, that the dust of his master's steps would settle directly on the disciple's body.

How many men today, instead, live by the motto: "Eat my dust!" as they climb the corporate ladder? Priorities, guys, priorities.

... Jesus said, "If you hold to my teaching, you are really my disciples. Then you will know the truth, and the truth will set you free" (John 8:31).

CONCLUSION:

This is the easy part. Given the above process of logic, pro/con lists, and Biblical support, it's a very simple conclusion. The priorities in life should look something like this:

1. **God:** We are His disciples and servants.
2. **Wife:** As husband we love, lead, serve, provide and protect.
3. **Kids:** As fathers we love, teach and discipline.
4. **Career:** We are to work to provide.

This should be the life we live, the life we model and the life we teach. But why is reality for so many a far cry from this idea? The answer to that question takes us back to Chapter 2, Dad vs. Culture.

If it's dad vs. culture, how do you counter this culture? Dave Simmons, in *Dad the Family Mentor*, says:

As mentor, you assume the responsibility to provide your children with the education they need. Strong fathers recognize they bear the responsibility for all facets of child education and stay involved in the total process. True, schools have taken the smothering burden of equipping our children with scholastic skills, but you must remember that they function under delegated authority. You are still accountable for your children.[4]

As you and your "delegated educators" equip your kids for career, remember proper perspectives on life. Mr. Simmons also implores:

...in child raising, we must avoid today's common problem of focusing exclusively on the child's personality, behavior, and skills without concentrating on the integrity of the heart. When we speak of teaching children, we need to begin with the topic of heart development before moving to personality, behavior, and skills.
Fatherhood helps a child develop a heart of integrity...[5]

You see, it is with the heart we seek God. It is with the heart we love our wives. If we turn our hearts to our children, they will turn their hearts to us (Malachi 4:6).

PRIORITIES IN EDUCATION

Imagine a bookcase sprawled from floor to ceiling, stretching the entire length of your living room. Imagine filling that bookcase with schoolbooks. At the far left, place your first preschool reader – the alphabet, basic one-syllable words, written with creative children's stories. Place every schoolbook you ever read, studied, highlighted, and from which were tested. At the far right, find your biggest, fattest, most expensive college textbooks. Just for fun, add your professional manuals and regulations. Books placed side-by-side, wall-to-wall, floor-to-ceiling.

Now on the opposing wall, imagine another bookcase. Place on that bookcase every book you ever read, studied, highlighted and from which your were tested – covering the subject of *fatherhood*. Go ahead and add your biggest, fattest, most expensive textbooks covering the subject of *marriage*. Give the books on the subject "*husband*" a shelf of their own. Don't forget all the graduate level textbooks on theology in your collection. Now stand back and take a look at the second bookcase. How big is it? How does it compare to the academic bookcase? And finally, how does this illustration relate with our life's priorities?

Robert Lewis:

"The typical young American male invests his time and energy in a bevy of self-centered activities – his career, his pleasures, his possessions – all the while believing they will matter beyond the moment.

This "conventional vision of manhood," as I call it, has five celebrated characteristics.

… it paints a one-dimensional picture, equating manhood with a "position."

… his value is earned; therefore, he becomes highly competitive.

… success is the goal – often at the expense of one's marriage, one's children, and meaningful, close relationships.

Fourth, *the reward of conventional manhood is power chiefly in the marketplace.*

And finally, *if a man becomes successful in this plan, he enjoys personal wealth and affluence.*"[6]

Don't sign me up for this "conventional vision." I'd rather take an eternal perspective. Howard G. Hendricks has more:

Most of us men have no problem asking the investment advice of a financial planner...
Most of us wouldn't hesitate to hire a golf pro to help us tame a slice...
Yet few of us would ever ask the advice of others on how to be a better father."
"The results of faithful fatherhood far outweigh any career climb, any economic windfall, or any position of power and fame that can be imagined.[7]

Finally, Dr. Lewis suggests we listen to the words of one of the world's foremost conventional men:

Anything I wanted, I took. I did not restrain myself from any joy. I even found great pleasure in hard work, an additional reward for all my labors. But as I looked at everything I had worked so hard to accomplish, it was all so meaningless. It was like chasing the wind. There was nothing really worthwhile anywhere. (written by King Solomon in Ecclesiastes 2:10-11)[8]

COMMITMENT

Ed Cole tells this story. Addressing a group of men of all ages, this is his account:

Looking eyeball to eyeball with thousands of young men, I asked point-blank, "Aren't there any young men of high school or college age who have the guts and courage to do more than wallow around in the moral morass of mediocrity to which so many have sunk?"
"Aren't there any young men who have guts and a love for God in their hearts, and enough of a desire

to serve God that they'll present their bodies to God, a living sacrifice which is their reasonable service?"

"Aren't there any who want the glory of God to be present in their lives through their virginity and in their decision for moral excellence?"

"Aren't there any young men anywhere who want to stand up for God, admit that they want to be 'men of God' and pay the price by developing a godly character?"

If there are...."

Before I could finish my statement, hundreds of young men leaped from their chairs and began to run for the front, some jumping onto the floor of that basketball arena, to race to center court where they stood, four hundred strong, declaring their allegiance to Jesus Christ.

As they ran, the other men stood and applauded them, some of them weeping as they watched these young men who were not ashamed to be called "men of God." It was explosive.

Thank God there are young men who have that burning desire to be outstanding men who are willing to pay the price for the true manhood which is Christlikeness – *single men who realize they need to grow and mature as men now, not wait until they are married.*

But, we need men who have a burning desire to *mentor* these young men, they can't do it on their own.[9] (*italics mine*)

No, they can't do it on their own. And it takes a special kind of man to fill the void. So what makes this kind of man? It's simple. As Sam Mahaffie points out, "Many dads are great mentors to their sons; those are the dads who have their *priorities* in order and who know the importance of making time for their boys"[10] (*italics mine*). And Steve Farrar can tell you what these priorities look like: "We need some men who have a passion to be better fathers than they are accountants. We need some men who have a passion to be better dads than they are attorneys, salesmen, foremen, pastors, or doctors. ... Are you one of these men? You can be!"[11]

I'M NOT QUALIFIED

I know; you may not feel qualified. You feel inadequate. This all sounds intimidating. There are certain qualities you'll need before you can step into this kind of teaching commitment, right? Consider this: "Very often, the only way to get a quality is to start behaving as if you had it already" (C.S. Lewis). You see, if you want to learn something, *teach it*. Don't think you have to become an expert before you teach. Just knowing young men are counting on you will give you the heart and desire to know what you're talking about and come through for them. With the right priorities in your life, you will come through for them with flying colors. In fact, without your mentorship, your boys, and others, will someday be in the same empty, unsatisfying, treadmill life that you may be in today. Only you and I can prevent that from happening. We must pass down *authentic manhood* to the next generation of men.

Chapter 5

Squires

It's been said, "The road to hell is paved with good intentions." With the busyness arranged for us by Satan (or that we've brought on to ourselves), the deceiver knows we'll probably keep those good intentions right where they are. And he's just fine with that. If we intend to mentor our sons into Biblical manhood, but are too busy and distracted to move forward with a deliberate plan, Satan is pleased.

In the previous chapters I have alluded to a mentoring plan that could transform good intentions into positive action. I first mentioned the *group* of men inquiring about the rite of passage sword and the 10% discount we received on an order of 15 swords. I told you about the "thing-in-the-box," the title given the secret object-lesson props for our introductory *group* meeting. Next, I cited the desperate need for mentoring of the fatherless. I suggested the need for a formalized *group*, with the necessary teaching vision and member commitment. I pounded in the idea of accountability within a small *group*. Finally, I told of a *group* of high school and college young men with a burning desire for Christ-like manhood and a need for men who have a burning desire to mentor these young men. This is where the rubber meets the road. It's going to be done in a *group* setting.

I liken it to getting a membership to a fitness center. Thinking the monthly payment would be the incentive to stick with an exercise routine, you sign up. But you're not getting your money's worth. It's not until you find an exercise partner that you finally stay consistent. As I said in Chapter 3, when you don't show up at the gym at the appointed time, there's something about that phone call from your partner at 5:05 a.m. that keeps you on task. Your partner keeps you honest. Imagine that same accountability from your fellow mentors.

The inspiring words of Robert Lewis describe this:

> Boys become men in the community of men. There is no substitute for this vital component. Dad, if your boy is to become a man, *you must enlist the community.* This is imperative for three reasons.
>
> First, if a father's presence is weighty, the presence of other men is weightier still.
>
> Second, enlisting the community of men results in a depth of friendship that the lonely never experience.
>
> And third, the community of men expands a son's spiritual and moral resources.
>
> Seek out a group of fathers with sons who will band together with you in the adventure.

He continues, "[most men are] shut up in the solitude of their own hearts. Other than the superficial "hellos" at work and the shallow conversations in the church foyer, many of us are disconnected from this life-giving organism we call 'the community of men.' We may not realize it, but we're suffering in its absence. And so are our sons."[1]

Why do we always try to go it alone, guys? Gary Smalley and John Trent, in a book chapter titled: "The Hidden Power of Friends," argue that even our health will benefit from the association with friends in small groups.[2] There are simply too many good reasons to ignore. We must join together with our friends (or our son's friend's dads) in mentoring the next generation of men.

Let us not give up meeting together, as some are in the habit of doing, but let us encourage one another - (Hebrews 10:25).

HOW TO STAY COMMITTED

I have already suggested the need for a *formalized group*. The most effective group format for Christ-centered manhood training is one that is dedicated just for that purpose. Building such a program from ground up is a significant commitment, but there are those of you prepared to take on such a commitment. I'll cover a detailed plan for this later, but first consider this:

Building such a program may be a bit much for most of us. Why build a program from scratch when there are many programs already in existence? They may be lacking in the manhood training element, but building a new program from ground up may not be necessary. A few good men willing to offer short Christ-centered manhood lessons could make a huge difference with these *existing* programs.

SUPPORT OTHER PROGRAMS

So you don't have to reinvent the wheel. Maybe you're already involved with youth Sunday School or Youth Group. Maybe your son is in the Boy Scouts and you're a registered leader. Maybe you coach a team sport and have the leeway to offer Christian truths to your team. The only element missing in these existing programs may be a focus on Christian Biblical manhood.

Church youth groups are usually co-ed, so they tend to fall short of defining manhood and of offering a masculine set of ideals. The Boy Scout program is not a Christian organization and falls short in the emphasis of God's design for family. But Boy Scout leaders are permitted to bring their religion into the program. Athletic programs teach teamwork and leadership, but lean too heavy on competitiveness, self-glory, and money. Your initiative and vision can supplement these existing athletic programs.

Step forward with your plan. Motivate the leaders with the issues I've shared in the first four chapters – rite of passage, culture, role modeling, mentoring, and mentoring priorities. Offer a Biblical perspective for the mentorship of the boys – a perspective that reveals the shortfalls of today's programs and even today's families.

These current programs are compatible with our vision for tomorrow's knights. You could offer some boys-only classes to the church Sunday School or Youth Group. These classes could be offered during the existing time slots or added as Sunday afternoon activities. They could be weekly or monthly. You could offer six-week semester classes just for the guys.

You could become the Boy Scout Troop Chaplain and offer a Chaplain's Minute after each troop meeting (plan on 5 to 10 minutes), expanding from the Scout Oath and Law with the Bible's teachings on manhood. Encourage the boys to earn the Boy Scout religious award, *God and Country*, and offer the necessary counseling for the award. Monthly campouts could include a church service that also teaches Christ-centered manhood. As a Troop Chaplain, you could mentor a youth Chaplain's Aid, guiding his leadership training with this teaching plan.

Even athletic teams can utilize a team chaplain and offer routine lessons and discussions for our purpose. Jeffrey Marx shares in his book, *Season of Life*, the story of ex-NFL football player Joe Ehrman. The story focuses on Joe's biblical manhood mentorship to a youth football team. In the book, Mr. Marx quotes Joe in a remark about our society: "We simply don't do a good enough job of teaching boys how to be men."[3] A team chaplain could teach a short devotional at each practice, focusing on – you guessed it, Christ-centered manhood.

I shared this with one of *my* current mentors, Neil Fisher. He offered a very relevant proposal. Because so many of our athletic programs are available through the public school system, a Christ-centered program may have to be student led. If the student athletes were encouraged to step forward with the proper resources, the vision of biblical manhood could be effectively shared to many young men who are out from under the umbrella of the church. The Fellowship of Christian Athletes (FCA) may be a great contact point for such a program. What an incredible hope for these young men.

Having said that, I have also discovered a program offered in public schools by a Christian ministry. Check out Tony Rorie's Men of Honor program at www.themenofhonor.org. Tony knows the ins and outs of after-school programs and how to offer Christ-centered teaching to public school kids.

Also, a ministry called "The Rev" forms Bible Clubs at public schools (go to www.therev.cc). By merely using the "club" label and soliciting a teacher sponsor these student-led groups have all the legal rights and privileges of any other student club.

DEDICATED MENTORING GROUP

Consider this: There is a modern movement known as "Futurism." By their name, one thing is obvious about Futurists – you guessed it, they look to the future. While there are some pretty crazy ideas about the future, there is one particular view that I'd like us to sink our teeth into. There are futurists who have concluded that our boys must be deliberately trained in the disciplines of becoming husbands and fathers. Futurists have taken a visionary look at our history and our present to anticipate the needs of the future; and they see a need for change, not in careerism, not in womanhood, but in manhood. Our future will need *authentic* manhood. Futurists believe that this authentic manhood must become a reality through a deliberate, intentional training plan.

Years ago, several of my son's grade school friends were missing a male role model in their lives. As I watched their fatherless scenarios played out, I felt drawn to get involved. It took about ten years from this first calling until I implemented a deliberate mentoring plan for my son and these young men.

So, for those ready to give your sons this type of dedicated manhood training, let's take a look at the necessary elements of a workable program and discover how each can fit you and your specific circumstances.

A GROUP ROSTER

First, invite a few others to join you and make a roster of names. You'd probably like your best friends involved, specifically those with sons. As I hinted once before, your son's friends and their dads are obvious choices as well. Among these men, you'd like at least one other man Biblically grounded and spiritually mature. As a side benefit to your vision for the boys, you may consider a father in need of mentorship himself, one struggling in *his* faith, in *his* manhood, or in *his* role as mentor to *his* son. Finally, reach out to one or two fatherless boys. I can't say enough about the need in this area.

As I have taught on the subject of mentoring boys, single moms are always among those interested in the subject. In each and every case, these moms find an opportunity to pull me aside and share *their* story. Tears well up in every one of these conversations. I have discovered that their interest is not so much in what they can do for their boys, but where to find men to step in on behalf of the missing father.

Sam Mehaffie shares a related story in *Every Man's a Mentor*. He tells of a gentleman out mowing his lawn a few years back. A neighboring single mom approached him and "She hesitated a little, then began to tell him of some problems she was having with her son ... She confided that he was acting differently and that she was just not sure what was going on in his life." The gentleman offered a neighborly commentary of concern and went back to his yard work.

Three years later, this same man was out mowing his lawn again. He stopped to get a drink of water when he noticed the now 16-year old boy from next door. He was really a messed up kid: bad attitude, bad language, listening to bad music, not treating his mom right. He had even heard the boy was into porn. "Too bad," he thought; his mind went back to that day three years earlier when his neighbor came over to talk about her son. He then realized that she had been asking for help, and he had not given it.[4]

These moms are fully aware of the "masculinity bestows masculinity" concept. They know they have a need; their sons have a need. The answer to their need is *you!*

So what size is right for your group? That's where individual needs and circumstances come in. Are you fired up to reach as many boys as you can? Go for it! Invite ten or twelve boys plus any men involved in the lives of these boys. Would you prefer a smaller, more intimate group: you, your best friend and your two sons? Fine. But don't forget your son's best friend and his dad. And I'll bet by now you've got a fatherless boy's name in mind. I've brought that up enough times; I'm sure you've thought of at least one in your circle of influence, so don't leave him out.

A GROUP NAME

Next, give your group a name. If you'd like to pick a name on your own, that's your prerogative. That's what I did. I had been inspired by the knighthood theme so much, with Robert Lewis' "modern-day knight," the Armor of God scriptures of Ephesians 6 and my son's rite of passage sword, I chose the title given an apprentice for knighthood. He was called a *squire*.

A squire of the medieval period started his training at the age of thirteen. During the five plus years of training, he had to prove himself a gentleman, a disciple of God, as well as a superior warrior. Then, when the king dubbed him a knight, all the people knew what he stood for, what his purpose was and whom he served.

I have even adopted this time-line for *our* mentoring plan. We started the group when the boys were about thirteen years old. We are committed to keep the group together and continue the formalized training until all the boys leave home (around high school graduation and about eighteen years old). This is a commitment of at least five years.

If you'd rather, you can wait to choose a group name until your first meeting and allow the guys to be involved in selecting a group name. This may help ensure the unity necessary for such a group. Let me share a story that addresses this name selection process, while also illustrating the relationship/authority balance introduced in Chapter 2.

KIDS KAMP STORY

I was the lead camp counselor for seventh grade boys at my church's summer Kids Kamp. The camp included second through seventh graders, so mine was the oldest group of boys. We were instructed to allow the group members to select a group name.

Now you'd think four macho men could handle a bunch of seventh grade boys. But boys who have not been taught to respect authority don't expect consequences for disrespectful behavior. So initially, the boys were rambunctious and disrespectful. With little cooperation, they seemed to be agreeing on the name: "Fat Boys." Discouraged at their behavior and their choice of group name, I insisted on getting their full attention and I overrode their name selection. First, I insisted on order and respect. Then I reminded them of the need for an appropriate Christian related theme for their group name; after all, this was church camp.

As we continued with our group name selection, each nomination continued with this "fat" theme, chubby this or tubby that. I didn't get it. I was at a complete loss as to what these boys were up to.

When I left the meeting, I was not at ease with the whole experience. As I shared my uneasiness with a few others; one finally asked, "You know what fat is, don't you?" Well, fat is fat, big, overweight. Right? Wrong!

I was told fat was spelled P-H-A-T. Pretty, Hot And Tempting. Those guys knew what they were getting away with. They also knew that the four of us men were clueless. They were ready to strut their stuff in front of the seventh grade girls, showing how *pretty hot and tempting* they were.

I couldn't let them prevail. These young guys were going to trample all over us counselors if we let them win. We would have no effect on them if they saw us as pushovers.

They were going to be totally distracted from the camp teaching topics as they focused on the girls across the room. I had to reestablish a proper position of relationship and authority for the four counselors.

I selected a new name for the group and planned a little meeting with the boys to take place just before we got on the buses. Each of the other counselors and the camp director were called for their approval.

When we had all gathered the morning of our trip to camp, I got the attention of all the boys. All of the parents were standing around to witness this meeting. I told the boys of our discovery of the PHAT theme and again reminded them of the obvious; this was church camp. Next, their disrespectful behavior was addressed and I explained that it would not be tolerated. I pulled out my son's Crusader sword and told of its significance (knighthood, the Armor of God). They thought that was pretty cool. I informed them we'd be called "Christ's Crusaders." The boys were then reminded that they were the oldest boys at the camp, *the men*, and would be looked up to by all of the other kids. Even the seventh grade girls would be watching them closely. I told them that the counselors knew they could live up to the expectations we set for them as *the men* of the camp.

Finally, I told the boys that when a counselor addressed them, they were to give him their undivided attention. No exceptions, no leniency, no tolerance of disrespect. When an adult counselor wanted their attention, he would yell out loud, "Crusaders!" When the boys heard this, they were to immediately stop what they were doing, turn in the direction of that counselor, and simultaneously yell, "Act Like Men!" I shared with them 1 Corinthians 16:13-14, "Be on your guard, stand firm in the faith, act like men; be strong. Do everything in love." This verse and specifically "act like men" would be our group theme. We then practiced this attention getting challenge and response. "Crusaders!" "ACT LIKE MEN!" "Crusaders!" "ACT LIKE MEN!" They were psyched! During the entire week of camp, every time we yelled that challenge and response, the whole camp looked in our direction. All eyes were on these boys. The boys knew what was expected of them and they came through wonderfully. Counselors and campers alike were commenting on the outstanding behavior of the seventh grade boys. I discovered years later that they nearly attempted a coup d'état over being required to let the girls eat ahead of them at every meal (I think they'll get the picture later in life), but the four men in charge reaped the benefit of relationship *with* these boys and authority *over* these boys.

SCHEDULE

The next planning issue for a mentoring group: decide on a routine schedule. Give everybody a schedule they can mark on their calendars. This will help keep other activities from bumping your group meetings out of their busy schedules (not completely, but it will help). Decide also how often you'll meet. Weekly would be ideal, but good luck fitting a weekly mentoring group into the array of school, athletic and other extracurricular activities that help kids get into colleges and earn scholarships. It's hard to compete with them. I have settled with a monthly meeting on the Sunday afternoon of every first full weekend of each month. We meet for about five hours in the afternoon after church and have committed to this schedule until the boys leave home some day. You should decide ahead of time how long you plan on meeting together. You may decide to initially commit to a year or even three months at a time, then reassess as you go.

MEETING PLACE

There is no limit to the variation for this part of your plan. You can meet at homes, churches, schoolyards, parks, gyms, ranches or other private acreage. When Steve Chapman offers *10 Things I Want My Son to Know* in his book by that name, he suggests, "From the backyard with little children to the remote mountains of faraway places with young adults, God's creation is an incredible way to inform kids about their Maker."[5]

Another element to add to your location is a campfire. Jeremy V. Jones shares this in an article titled *Bonding in the Backcountry*: "There's nothing quite like a campfire to get men talking. Starring into glowing embers beneath a canopy of stars has a way of moving a man's soul beyond the mundane and onto the ultimate issues of life. Even the most tight-lipped male may find himself steeped in discussion deep into the night."[6]

Our Squires group meets at a sixteen acre private home with open country surrounding the property. We have open fields, thick woods, a wet weather creek and a spot for a large campfire. I understand this option is not available to everyone. However, I have found that the more people I share our mentoring story with, the more resources are offered to me to use for this wonderful cause. Talk around and you may be surprised at what people may offer. God can provide.

A FORMAL COMMITMENT

This is the last, but possibly the most important element of the plan. As much as possible, every individual, from youth to adult, must make a formal pledge to stay committed to the group and to the vision. Inform the single moms of the level of commitment you are making to her son and the commitment you expect from him (and her). Specifically ask her to help her son stay the course. Consider putting this pledge in writing and expecting all participants to sign. Periodic reminders will be required to help keep the commitment level up.

Keep in mind, not all are likely to persevere. So much of our culture draws us into a harried schedule; many scheduling conflicts will arise for most involved. Often, we are so distracted with life's activities; many plans get forgotten – left off the calendar. Lack of organizational skills may also be the culprit for the absence of many.

There are some creative ways to help your fellow mentors and squires stay committed. I have found periodic phone contact to be most effective. This works well for a small group. For larger groups, email reminders may prove to be effective, although many do not have or check email. RSVPs are helpful; you know who plans on coming or not. You also know by a lack of response, which members could use a special call as a reminder and encouragement. You can encourage the adult men to stay involved just by telling them how much you appreciate their participation. Finally, some of the young men may become disinterested and pull away from their commitment to the group. If you continue to reach out to these youth, even when they seem disinterested, you may be the one they turn to when they need someone down the road. Perseverance is key.

EXECUTING THE PLAN

The first issue – who's in charge? Well, you're probably the guy initiating this whole thing, so I guess that's you. But I'll tell you what, you might consider calling yourself "the facilitator" and expect the other men to take turns planning, leading and teaching. I think this shared leadership by the men communicates to the boys that all of the men are in this together – each with a vested interest, each with a bit of wisdom and experience to offer. If you share the leadership burden, a monthly routine would require each of you to plan, lead and teach three or four times a year, depending on the number of men involved and the frequency of meeting.

ACTIVITES

Each meeting should include a planned activity that will bond men and boys together. The boys will look forward to the meetings, eager to rough it up and get dirty, compete and take risks, and most importantly, bond as men. For Boy Scout meetings and team sport practices, this type of activity is already built into the program.

In a conversation I had with Robert Lewis, I shared this activity element of our Squires mentoring plan. He responded by highlighting a need for these kinds of *common experiences* between father and son, mentor and protégé. He explained how these common experiences create memories that burn the manhood lessons into their long-term memory. They never forget the vision born out of these experiences.

We will spend an entire chapter covering "Guy Kinda Fun" later.

SET OF IDEALS

A well-defined set of ideals is very important. It gives direction to your mentoring plan, it facilitates moment-by-moment teaching and it defines day-to-day behavior. Your group's set of ideals (code of conduct, character traits, masculine roles; whatever you want to call them) will be your group's foundation. This is the missing element for *Christ-centered manhood training* needed in our team sports programs, Youth Groups, and even the Boy Scouts. It will set parameters, establish expectations, define roles, create a common language, and guide you and your boys together.

Where will you get this foundational element for your group? While there are endless resources for this, God's Word must be the rock that gives your set of ideals proper Biblical perspective. I'll offer several sources for your consideration and then offer the teaching plan I've used in our Squires group. So let's take a look at a few ideas.

BOY SCOUT OATH AND LAW[7]

"Trustworthy, loyal, helpful, friendly..." I'm sure many of us can recite these twelve points of the Scout Law by memory. The Scout Oath points a boy to God and country, to service and morality, and to twelve character traits outlined in the Scout Law. The Boy Scouts of America is a wonderful program. They offer outstanding resources, training and vision. Members of the Boy Scouts are required to be reverent to God – any god. And this where a Christian must be cautious. Although many of the charter organizations sponsoring Boy Scout troops are Christian churches, the BSA is not a Christian organization. Involvement in Boy Scouts and embracing the Scout Oath and law must be supplemented with a focus on *the* God, the Father of Jesus Christ. Also, while this program promotes faith, good citizenship and leadership, it may be considered lacking in it's training for *family* leadership.

PROMISE KEEPERS

Promise Keepers guides men with the *Seven Promises of a Promise Keeper*. This outstanding men's ministry offers exciting stadium events for revival and excellent programs for ongoing growth. They have published a book titled *Seven Promises of a Promise* Keeper,[8] drawing from the wisdom and experience of numerous co-authors. I recommend you look into what they have to offer. Go to www.promise-keepers.org.

RAISING A MODERN-DAY KNIGHT, ROBERT LEWIS[9]

Robert Lewis' *Raising a Modern-Day Knight* has obviously inspired me. It is a must read. When I invited a group of men and boys to meet together, forming a second mentoring group, several men described this group as an answer to prayer. They had read Dr. Lewis' book and had shared a vision to follow his advice. Without hesitation, they said, "We're in!"

In his book, Dr. Lewis offers four manhood principles, three responsibilities of a man, and a code of conduct. In chapter 3, A Vision for Manhood, he quotes from 1 Corinthians 16:13. I latched on to that verse and made it the benchmark for our Squires mentoring group. Go to www. RMDK.com.

WHAT THE BIBLE SAYS ABOUT ... BEING A MAN, J. RICHARD FUGATE[10]

Well, the title sure works for me. I jumped right into his text and loved it. Mr. Fugate is concise, direct, to the point, and Biblically sound. He offers four key functions of a Biblical man, characteristics of a leader, and roles defined by God for man.

FIVE STEPS TO MANHOOD, DENNIS RAINEY[11]

Some time ago, I received an audiocassette from Family Life Ministries. It presents Dennis Rainey's vision for manhood. In it, he offers five superb steps, taking a lad from boyhood and helping him progress to the senior stage as patriarch.

BRINGING UP BOYS, JAMES DOBSON[12]

Another inspiring resource is the award winning, record setting *Bring Up Boys*, by Dr. James Dobson. This book and its author have offered endless advice, encouragement and wisdom to our nation. From his text, I found Dr. Dobson's view on men's roles as provider, protector, leader, and spiritual mentor.

These are but a few of the resources available to you. With little effort, you could find a tremendous assortment of additional resources. Some other outstanding books I've read include: *The Hidden Value of a* Man, by Gary Smalley and John Trent, *Point Man*, by Steve Farrar, *Tender Warrior*, by Stu Weber, *The Christian Husband*, by Bob Lepine, *Family Man, Family Leader*, by Phillip Lancanster, *A Man's Touch*, by Charles Stanley, *Dad the Family Mentor*, by Dave Simmons, and *The Father Connection*, by Josh McDowell. And while we struggle to protect our precious time, books on CD are ideal for an otherwise total waste of time – the drive to work.

But you may have already embraced a set of ideals for yourself and your son. Or you may want to pursue your own vision from what you've learned here. Let me share the direction I have taken. And I'll explain why I chose my plan.

KNIGHTHOOD VERSES

As I pursued a deliberate training plan, three Bible verses seemed to emerge as comprehensive references. Combined, they covered all of the relevant manhood roles and responsibilities offered by the above books and authors. From these scriptures I call Knighthood Verses, I derived a list of twelve teaching topics, or character traits, as our "set of ideals." They are wisdom, stature, favor with God, favor with men, being on your guard, standing firm in the faith, to act like men, being strong, being doers, doing everything in love, borne of sinful man – to bear the likeness of Christ.

The beauty of this plan is found in the direct reference to scripture memorization. Some wise or experienced man didn't compile the verbiage of this list; it is directly from God's Word.

LUKE 2:52

Our first verse is often used for motivating teenagers to engage in their Christian faith. Luke 2:52 wraps up a story about the boy, Jesus. But it also introduces a subsequent chapter in His life. *"And Jesus grew in wisdom and stature, and in favor with God and men."* It is the growth during His teen years that makes this verse relevant to mentoring our boys.

The relevance and its implication for teens today actually centers on two facts. First, verse 42 states that Jesus was twelve years old at the time of this story. As we've seen, this is a great age to prepare our son's rite of passage and begin his formal manhood training. Second, the specific growth described in this passage sets the stage for Jesus' ministry. God had a specific plan for His Son and prepared Him through this growth. And God has a plan for your son, too.

Drawing from the specifics of Luke 2:52, we have four teaching topics. I consider these four attributes to be "the fundamentals" of growing up as a Christian. We must teach our son *wisdom* from above. We must further his *stature* through proper diet and physical activity. We must promote his faith in Jesus and his walk with God, helping him grow in *favor with God*. And we must teach him to relate properly with people in order to gain *favor with men* – to God's glory, not his own.

1 CORINTHIANS 16:13-14

The second verse offers a more advanced approach to your son's maturing process. With three powerful words buried right in the middle, this passage also offers a central theme for mentorship into manhood – *act like men*. 1 Corinthians 16:13-14 (adopted from NIV and NASB): "*Be on your guard, stand firm in the faith, act like men; be strong. Do everything in love.*" At first glance, you might see five teaching topics. I'll point out a sixth.

Be on your guard; powerful advice for facing temptations from the world, from Satan and from your "own evil desire" (James 1:14). *Stand firm in the faith*; the ongoing life of discipleship and servant-hood to God. *Act like men*; our central theme. From this, we address our roles and responsibilities as disciple, servant, husband, father, patriarch, spiritual leader, servant leader, provider and protector. In this directive from Paul, the original text refers to a masculine *courage*. *Be strong*, a masculine trait for blessing the women and children in our lives. *Do everything in love*; the hidden topic "Do" - offering an exhortation to be *doers* – proactive rather than passive or reactive. "*Everything in love*" sums up the law; love the Lord and love your neighbor (and even love your enemy).

1 CORINTHIANS 15:49

Each believer must grasp the contradicting realities of his identity in the world and his identity *in Christ*. From this understanding comes a "walk by the Spirit" that is released from the burden of works-based faith. "*Just as we have borne the likeness of the earthly man, so shall we bear the like-*

ness of the man from heaven." Our last two teaching topics cover our natural character, from Adam, and our spiritual character, from Christ. While the gospel story tells of our justification through faith in Jesus Christ, the rest of the story tells of our faith-based longing for the nature and character of God – Christ-likeness.

See the Appendix for expanded explanations of the twelve teaching topics.

TEACHING TOOLS

Once you have established a set of ideals, *memorize them.* Help and encourage all involved to do the same, men and boys alike. With your set of ideals, you will have a common reference for guiding your boys toward Biblical manhood.

In my interview with Robert Lewis, he referred to our use of manhood reference words as a *"common language."* These are words generally not in the normal vocabulary of young men, words like *manhood, spiritual leader, wisdom, and courage.* Wait a minute – these are words generally not in the vocabulary of today's older men either. But once you have developed a common manhood language with your sons, mentoring can happen with hardly an effort or thought. Even the *vision* of Christ-centered manhood becomes ingrained in the boys through the routine use of your new *language.* The common language used by the boys and men in my Squires group is drawn directly from the three verses described above as well as from the expanded explanations I have offered our group.

With your new common language, you can plan group discussions covering the topics in your set of ideals. You can instruct your son with purpose. You can teach with authority, and in your teaching you can "show integrity, seriousness and soundness in speech that cannot be condemned..." (Titus 2:8).

The next step entails obtaining teaching resources. Just as in your search for a set of ideals, minimal effort will bring about a tremendous assortment of resources for your teaching topics. A curriculum is a good way to get started. For a nominal cost, you can take advantage of somebody else's time and effort. In it, you will likely find scriptural support, applicable real-life or fictitious stories, and activities that play out the lesson at hand. Be careful to avoid using the curriculum as a crutch. This may result in dry delivery and unresponsive participation.

Another approach to group learning is seen in book clubs. Each group member can read an assigned book over a prescribed time frame. Discussion can center on a specific chapter or topic from the book. This can be done informally or utilizing a study guide or workbook associated with the book.

My favorite method for teaching came with experience. I observed and discovered first hand the flat disposition of a teacher reading directly from a curriculum script. Eventually, I learned to prepare a curriculum lesson by initially reading just the support scriptures for the lesson. I would then pray and meditate on the topic and consider the particular kids participating in the class - their issues, behaviors, struggles, etc. I looked to the Holy Spirit for guidance and the Word for His wisdom. By the time I reviewed the actual lesson plan, I had somewhat of a plan already in my own mind. I considered the lesson plan activities, usually adding a bit of pizzazz with creative physical activity, a bit of humor, and extensive props. With enough experience from this practice, I eventually felt comfortable planning my own lessons. The beauty of this method is realized in the contagious demeanor of teaching from your own heart.

I am working with a team of men at Squires2Knights Ministries. We are creating resources for group mentorship, offering free references designed for group devotions and six-week courses in Christ-centered manhood. They are formatted for use in virtually any small group of young men and are specifically designed for teenagers. While they are a work-in-progress, the current resources can be found on www.Squires2Knights.com as downloadable files. Or better yet, weather resistant hard copies for outdoor use can be ordered free of charge. These resources have been prepared directly from our three Knighthood Verses.

Also look to the future for a devotional book for teen boys titled *A Squire's Devotional*. It will be available on www.SquiresToKnights.com. And as I mentioned earlier, my son and I are co-writing a book about Christ-centered manhood. It will present the lessons I have taught him as well as his perspective on the learning process.

RESPECT

A final point for the group mentoring method: It is paramount that proper behavior expectations be made absolutely clear. Respect from the boys must be established from the get go. A line should be drawn, defining acceptable behavior, establishing authority, and promoting respect for property. This line should define black from white, little or no gray area. These expectations should be accompanied by realistic consequences for noncompliance - consequences to be carried out with consistency.

I have experienced the frustration of working with boys when the adult leaders did not know how (or chose not to) establish clear behavior expectations and consistently enforce them. In fact, the Boy Scouts spelled out the expectations for them, but the adult Scout Masters were ill equipped to stand firm with consistent enforcement. The boys learned quickly which restrictions were not enforced and thereby, didn't really apply. They even learned how to manipulate the adults and could get away with almost anything. My attempts at enforcement only caused confusion for the boys and lead to an improper balance of relationship and authority.

Eventually, a move to a new Scout troop illustrated the significance of this issue. The new troop adult leadership had a completely different approach to behavior expectations and accountability. Their clarity and consistency made a world of difference - a difference that promoted true mentorship.

As you establish expectations, servant-hood should be the name of the game. Remember, "love" sums up the law and is the central theme for behavior expectations. Big Joe Ehrmann tells his high school football players that his job as their coach is to love them and their job as players is to love each other. How's that for unconventional coaching? HBO even featured Joe and his coaching style On Real Sports with Bryant Gumball. But imagine the team cohesiveness under that philosophy.

If these behavioral boundaries are established early and enforced consistently, every aspect of your group mentoring effort will benefit. The boys don't consciously know this, but they want these boundaries and want to know that someone is in charge.

> Young men, in the same way be submissive to those who are older (1 Peter 5:5).

If you're going to demand respect, you must first *command* respect. There's a big difference. Commanding respect is different than ordering someone to respect you. It means you must act in a manner deserving respect. Sam Mehaffie offers this reality:

> Even though they may not act like it, kids today are very teachable. They want advice and guidance, but they will not listen to just anyone. They will only listen to someone they respect. We need to be the

men whom our boys look up to and *respect*; otherwise we will not be able to reach them. It is the only
way boys can be discipled by us to become the men
God intended them to be.[13] (*italics mine*)

One final point, by Josh McDowell, with regard to
respect: "One of the keys to becoming a father who is worthy
of respect is being a father who *shows* respect, just as God
the Father not only commands respect but shows it to us as
well."[14]

SOMETHING IN COMMON

Often, the roadblock for relationship between the generations is described this way: "We have nothing in common."
Robert Lewis shared with me three words that help me describe
the solution to this problem: experience, language, and vision.
When he put the word *common* in front of those three words
I had the perfect explanation for how and why the group-
mentoring plan works so well. Create common experiences, a
common language, and a common vision for Christ-centered
manhood - men and boys alike will discover together God's
plan for them. As John Eldredge shares, "We need a process,
a journey, an epic story of many experiences woven together,
building upon one another in a progression."[15]

KNIGHT IN SHINING ARMOR

Imagine a beautiful maiden waiting for her knight in
shining armor. She longs for a man of courage and integrity,
a true gentleman, a Godly man. One who has persevered as
a squire, now fully trained as a knight.

Does this young man exist only in fairy tales? No – he is
real, he is relevant, he is our future. And he is in your hands
today.

Commit to God's plan, to time-honored tradition – to mentorship. Commit to your son, to other fathers and sons; commit to the fatherless.

Teach Christ-centered manhood to the boys on the team, in the troop, at the school or at church. Or create a formalized mentoring program that rivals (if not surpasses) your best project at work. Then *execute*.

Chapter 6

Guy Kinda Fun!

Picture this:

- BANG! You're dead!

- No I'm not!

- Yes you are. I shot you.

- You missed.

- No I didn't.

- Yes you did.

What's going on here? What mental image do you have of this scenario? I'll bet you envision two boys. You probably imagine them to be around ten years old and you picture them, no doubt, in jeans and t-shirts. They have toy guns in their hands and are hiding behind a tree or bush as they battle it out.

What you *didn't* envision was two teenage girls - in dresses, their hair done up nice, a purse in one hand and a toy gun in the other, as they battle it out in the mall foyer. No, this kind of play is generally a *guy* thing. That's not to say that girls don't play Army or "Cowboys and Indians." But as evidenced by your mental image of the above scenario, we all see this as "guy kinda fun."

In fact, I remember reading about a study a long time ago. The researchers used toddlers who were unable to talk yet. The boys and girls were separated for this study and they were observed as they played. The findings were quite interesting. Every sound that came from the mouths of the girls was a mimicked form of speech - gibberish. They pretended to talk to each other. Their play incorporated imaginary relationships through communication. The boys, on the other hand, made very different sounds. Every sound out of their mouths was a sound-effect – a bang, thud, roar, or a swoosh. Their play was loud; it was action-based.

TESTOSTERONE FOR "GUY KINDA FUN"

We already know that testosterone is more prevalent in males than in females. We also know that this hormone has significant effects on the sexes making them quite different from each other. James Dobson points out for us that testosterone is clearly correlated with "psychological dominance, confident physicality and high self-esteem." He quotes Andrew Sullivan, "In most combative environments, especially physical ones, the person with the most [testosterone] wins."[1]

A single-mom e-mailed me once about a situation with her son. She had another mom of a neighbor boy come to her door. This mother was upset because the two boys had gotten into a fight. My friend's son apparently had hit her son, obviously an unacceptable outcome from her point of view. My friend was at odds as to what to do about her son's behavior. She was appalled with this physical fighting and was at her wits end.

As is common for single mothers of boys, much of the typical boy behavior is confusing. James Dobson's *Bringing Up Boys* has been a blessing to these mothers. He explains so much about boys, their temperament and behavior, giving these mothers a better understanding of their sons. So I shared with my friend the above facts about testosterone and it's influence, specifically as it relates to dominance, confidence, physicality and self-esteem. I quoted, "In most combative environments, especially physical ones ...," then I emphasized, "the person with the most wins" (referring to testosterone, of course). Then to offer some comic relief (she needed something to relieve the stress) I told her, "Next time this mother comes to your door accusing your son of hitting her son, tell her [with sarcasm], 'My son has more than yours.'"

Obviously, boys need to be taught appropriate responses when in disagreement with friends. I did not condone fighting and I emphasized that fighting is generally not acceptable. But my friend *did* need to understand that she was not dealing with some out-of-control severe behavioral problem. She was merely dealing with a *boy*. She didn't need to take the "boy" out of him, she needed to channel his natural behavior into appropriate conduct. The testosterone-induced behavior, when properly directed, would give him healthy masculine characteristics fit for God's design for him as a man. How's that for a controversial statement? But we're not looking for political correctness here. James Dobson offers this, "That brings us back to our understanding of boys. Remember that they are men-in-training. Their aggressive nature is designed for a purpose. It prepares them for the "provision and protection" roles to come."

MORE FROM TESTOSTERONE

Dr. Dobson declares more about the effects of testosterone:

> Most experts believe boys' tendency to take risks, to be more assertive, to fight and compete, to argue, to boast, and to excel at certain skills, such as problem solving, math, and science, is directly linked to the way the brain is hardwired and to the presence of testosterone.

Then he adds the following to the list, "They value change, opportunity, risk, speculation, and adventure."[2]

We can also glean from John Eldridge's perspective. In *Wild at Heart* he asserts, "The recipe for fun is pretty simple raising boys: Add to any activity an element of danger, stir in a little exploration, add a dash of destruction, and you've got yourself a winner." He goes on, "… adventure is written into the heart of man. And it's not just about having 'fun.' Adventure *requires* something of us, puts us to the test. Though we may fear the test, at the same time we yearn to be tested, to discover that we have what it takes."[3]

John Eldridge has something to say about our typical responses to boyish behavior. "I've noticed that so often our word for boys is *don't*. Don't climb on that, don't break anything, don't be so aggressive, don't be so noisy, don't be so messy, don't take such crazy risks." I have often seen Boy Scout adult leaders yelling, "Don't run!" and, "Stop jumping!" Go figure. They might as well establish a rule that says, "Don't act like a boy." Get real.

Mr. Eldridge has more: "But God's design – which he placed in boys as the picture of himself – is a resounding *yes*. Be fierce, be wild, be passionate. Now, none of this is to diminish the fact that a woman bears God's image as well. The masculine and feminine run throughout all creation."[4]

MASCULINE THRILLS

So, according to James Dobson and John Eldridge the best group activities for boys and men involve the masculine thrills of *adventure, competition, physicality, danger and destruction, exploration and an element of risk.* Not that we need two experts to tell us that, but they definitely confirm what we already know.

Why do you think boys and their fathers can be so dedicated to sports? Most of America's youth team sports bring all of the above elements of masculine thrills in a ready-made program. Just sign up, pay your fee, buy your uniform, and you're in. The Boy Scout program accomplishes the same goal. The program, with its camping, hiking, and assorted other outdoor activities, is already up and running. Join a troop and share the experience with your son.

So how does one mix these ingredients into "guy kinda fun" for just a few buddies – a *small group*? I described the following activities to a class of parents studying Dobson's *Bringing Up Boys.* Before I finished, a mom stopped me. She said, "Look around the room. Every man is leaning forward and sitting on the edge of his seat as they hear these stories." Here is what I shared - they are some of the activities we have used in our Squires mentoring group:

Air rifle shooting: Target shooting with a BB gun or pellet gun is certainly fun. But there's no action. There's no risk. We did a little target shooting to get warmed up, and then added some intensity to the activity. I tied five Coke cans to low lying branches hidden in the back woods of my property. I sent teams of two out along the property boundary, one man and one boy, timing them as they worked the perimeter, searching for the concealed targets. They had to find the cans (not knowing how many), shoot them from the boundary trail and reach a finish line as quickly as they could. Missing cans and violating safety rules resulted in time penalties. They were given only ten pellets each. The pressure to expedite and the need to find and shoot each target raised the competition to a new level.

My brother, a former army soldier, took his assignment in this backyard activity very serious. By the last target, he was asking for timing updates while he utilized Army marksman techniques to maximize his shooting accuracy.

Archery: Again, target shooting was a mere warm up. We then tied a target (a paper filled box) to a zip line with the archers lined up for its pass. With that, we were striving to hit a moving target!

Paintball: This sport has all of the elements boys love – competition, physicality, and risk. Boys have a natural desire to fulfill the role of protector. Role-play with guns is, therefore, inevitable for boys. If they are not provided opportunities for this role-play, they will invent their own, making an imaginary gun out of a stick, other toy, their hand, or even their peanut butter and jelly sandwich. And, if safety is a concern, a well-supervised and well-behaved group can follow the safety rules.

During one of our games, a dad had his first opportunity to play paintball. In the middle of the game, Glen moped his way out of the thicket of woods with his left forearm raised. It seems he didn't have time to clear the ground ahead of him as he attempted to dive out of a spray of paintballs. Landing on his belly with his left arm straddling a cactus, he felt the sting of a busted paintball on his side, of cactus needles in his arm, and the sting of defeat on his ego.

Our version of **Capture the Flag** features a single guard (me) standing in one position, protecting a flag placed nearby. We play this game at night and I use a million candle-watt spotlight. But I don't use the light as a searchlight; I use it as my weapon. If I see an enemy with my naked eyes, I shine the beam of light on him, killing him and making him return to his base to regenerate. The boys (and adult men) must strategize, covertly maneuver, camouflage, and navigate through the woods to sneak by me and capture the flag. They love it.

One evening, following a game of capture the flag, Darwin, a dad in his fifties discovered he had lost his glasses. He was sure he had lost them under a tree next to our campfire. We searched and searched to no avail. I finally suggested we wait till morning when it was light. My son and I would have better luck then.

When our search the next morning came up empty, I asked my son where Darwin was during the game of capture the flag. My son explained how Darwin had low-crawled ahead of him in an old cattle corral. So we returned to the place, not far from where I was guarding the flag, where Darwin, our mature adult competitor, had dared the elements (cactus, snakes, scorpions) to win the game. There, in the grass, we found his glasses.

Men never grow out of their boyhood fun.

Construction equipment: I had upwards of 50 yards of dirt piled up in my back yard following the construction of our house. I also have a friend with a skid-loader and a tracked excavator. I put those two facts together with a need for a mentoring group activity. The result was half a dozen teenagers taking turns learning how to operate this heavy equipment to move the dirt where I wanted it. Walla – cheap labor.

Wood cutting: Much of our group's teaching is done after sunset around a campfire. Campfires need wood. And what a great activity for a bunch of guys to do – cutting and splitting firewood. Guys can do it for hours – and enjoy it. In fact, I often had to ask the adult men to give up an ax to let the boys have a chance to cut.

Teaching around a **campfire:** Although not always, this is our preferred venue for teaching. We roast hotdogs over the fire, eat, *then* talk (they have a hard time eating and listening at the same time). I prepare a lesson and get the men and boys to participate in a discussion.

Frisbee Golf or Ultimate Frisbee: Easy and inexpensive.

Service Projects: Community Bible Church had been moving furniture, household goods and food goods from contributors, through a warehouse, to the Katrina hurricane evacuees in San Antonio. We offered this service through volunteers from the church. When I offered to bring 15 to 20 men and teenage boys to work for a few hours, rather than sorting canned goods, toilet paper, and diapers, the coordinator had visions of moving vans being loaded at the warehouse and then unloaded at an apartment complex. So we turned masculine muscle strength and endurance into a machine of provision. We delivered furniture to empty apartment living rooms and bedrooms for those who lost everything and had taken up temporary or permanent residence in San Antonio.

Short-term Missions Trips: My vision for these boys is to have them work together for Christ in an area of considerable need. My goal for them is to experience the blessings of service and evangelism on a mission trip. I want them to experience "favor with God and men," to "stand firm in the faith," and "do everything in love" as they "bear the likeness of the man from heaven."

Many of these activities require certain resources. The most obvious would be the need for a good chunk of private land. Certain equipment is also needed for many of the activities. These resources are not available to everybody. But keep in mind, the above activities are primarily offered to illustrate creative ways for planning "Guy Kinda Fun." Discover the favorites for *your* boys and then create your own activities. Or join an existing program with built-in "Guy Kinda Fun." And finally, as you share your mentoring experiences with others, you will find that God will provide additional resources. People will hear your stories and be inspired to offer their resources for such a worthy cause for Christ.

Chapter 7

Rule of Compound Return

No doubt, you've seen an illustration of the rule of compound return on investment? A simple comparison of money tucked away in a jar verses an interest bearing investment. The example validates the impact of compound return. First, the illustration demonstrates the results of saving, say, $1000 per year. After ten years, $10,000 is accumulated. After fifty years - $50,000.

Next, the illustration demonstrates the results of growth on an interest bearing investment. The simple interest on an annually invested $1000 over fifty years, at 10% per year, culminates to become $177,500. But the rule of *compound* return on an annual interest rate of 10%, adds up to 1.28 million dollars. Not bad.

INVESTING WITH AN ENTREPRENEURIAL SPIRIT

Let's take this rule of compound return and add to it a touch of creativity and discipline. An entrepreneurial investor could save his $1000 per year, invest the money at the long-term average interest rate of 10%, and *then* add an additional token amount of money. If he added a mere $200 per year (realized by drawing a small income from a hobby, let's say writing or painting or woodwork or teaching piano or photography or graphics design or – you get the picture), he would accrue a portfolio equal to 1.54 million. That's an additional $260,000 realized from the proceeds of a hobby. Now, let's say our investor then saved $10,000 every five years by purchasing a used car instead of a new car (and invested the savings). After fifty years, this creative and disciplined investor could accrue as much as 3.63 million dollars from the same nominal sacrifice of $1000 per year. That's almost three times that of the above basic fifty year savings plan with compound return – just by enjoying a hobby and driving a used car.

WHAT DOES THIS HAVE TO DO WITH MENTORING BOYS?

I am so encouraged by how God has moved through Christian ministries in our country and throughout the world. We are seeing His blessings in churches, in communities, in homes, even in politics. Organizations like Focus on the Family, Promise Keepers and Campus Crusade for Christ are glorifying God with the fruit of evangelism and ministry. Every soul saved increases His kingdom and every life changed bears fruit for Him. We are investing in God's people with a compounded return.

Let me explain how I believe God can move through us with *the* most effective fruit bearing ministry possible (entrepreneurial, if you will). I believe that no other target group for Christian ministry can have the same compound results (barring the intervening power of the Holy Spirit) than *today's boys*. Our next generation of men, raised from today's generation of boys, can bring about a change that honors God's plan for families, churches, communities, and our nation. This God honoring ministry has the potential for compound returns just as our creative and disciplined entre-preneurial investor did with his hobby, used cars and his $1000 per year.

Now, I can hear the grumblings under your breath already. This may give the appearance that I believe we would do this in our *own* power. This sounds like God's hand is not needed in this ingenious plan. I even offered the caveat: *"barring the intervening power of the Holy Spirit."* But you know what? I believe God is waiting for our obedience to Him and our heart for His plan. This "manhood" ministry would be a total contrast with today's legacy of men – careerism, mate-rialism, affluence, and missing in action at home.

I believe that a movement by today's men, raising the next generation of men, would be the *result* of the power of the Holy Spirit. This kind of obedience from men would glorify God and bring compounded blessing as prophesied in Malachi 4:5-6, "He will restore the hearts of the fathers to their children and the hearts of the children to their fathers." The Holy Spirit would be an invited guest and His power would be manifested through men who mentor today's boys. And just as is illustrated by the above entrepreneurial invest-ment plan, we can paint a picture of the rule of compound return that exceeds anything we've seen through our contem-porary Christian ministries. A tall order and a bold claim – so stay tuned.

CAN'T TEACH AN OLD DOG NEW TRICKS

I'll start with three simple points. First, men are pretty much set in their ways. It's hard to affect change in their lives. This leaves families with many work-a-holic men who fall short of fulfilling God's plan for them at home.

Second, boys are impressionable. They look to their role models and are willing to learn from mentors. All they need are mentors to provide the right kind of manhood training.

Third, while men are set in their ways, they *can* change. They just need the right kind of push. Men's ministries are affecting change in men all across our country. But I am convinced that if men believe their boys need them, if they understand the threats on their boys, if they know what their boys can accomplish through their fatherly mentorship, *men will come through.* This could be the most effective way to change men – *make them mentors.*

According to Robert Lewis, "Men assume social responsibility most naturally and effectively when (1) it is clear to them that the primary responsibility for the well-being of others rests on them and that others are relying on them, and (2) when they have been trained from an early age by the men in their lives to recognize and assume that responsibility faithfully."[1] Part one of his statement is fulfilled by making men into mentors. Part two becomes a reality for the next generation of men when today's men realize part one.

Now get ready for a ride across the pages of some wonderful books written by many of the most trusted Christian authors. Let's take a look at the compound return on investment into the next generation of men. Who will benefit?

THE NEXT GENERATION OF MEN

The target group of mentoring today's boys will obviously become the next generation of men. The time invested in them will bring about a new legacy for men in our nation. They will become better disciples and servants for God. The will become loving husbands and dedicated fathers. They will expand their influence to their grandchildren and beyond, their churches, communities, and our nation. They will lead, provide and protect. They will become all that God intended them to be, all because of our obedience to God's generational vision.

Dad the Family Mentor, Dave Simmons:

This process is what parenting is all about: the transfer of civilization from one generation to the next. Parents play the role of teachers, and children play the role of learners. Perhaps a word that describes the whole process is *absorption*: The new generation absorbs the old one.[2]

Manhood, taped presentation by Dennis Rainy:

Men suffer from two problems:

1. Lack of convictions about what it means to be a man.
2. At a loss to give a generational vision to our sons.[3]

Harold Davis, Champaign, IL

"When an older generation of men does not reach down and call the younger generation up, that generation perishes."[4]

Psalm 45:16:

Your sons will take the place of your fathers; ...

Psalm 24:6:

Such is the generation of those who seek him, who seek your face, O God of Jacob.

THE NEXT GENERATION OF FATHERLESS MEN

I cannot emphasize enough: the fatherless boys of today need Godly men in their lives. The number of boys in this category is astronomical and growing. They are the products of a systemic breakdown of manhood that has evolved over several previous generations. This breakdown of Godly manhood has created a pattern of divorce and single parenting that is outside God's plan. In turn, this growing problematic pattern is passed from one generation to another. The pattern must be broken.

My parents are examples of a resolute desire to break the pattern. My father, as a twelve-year-old, lost his dad to a stroke and was then raised entirely by his single mother. My mother overcame the burden of an absent father and two abusive stepfathers. My parents came together in marriage and modeled for me, and my siblings, a marital and parenting commitment that I hold dear. The pattern was broken and I want to help break this pattern in the lives of others who are not so fortunate.

Bringing Up Boys, James Dobson

Since remarriage may or may not solve the problem of finding masculine influence for her boys, the single mother has to figure out other ways to meet the challenge. How can she teach them to … think like a man? What can she tell them about male sexuality, and what can she do to get them ready to lead future families of their own?

[God] said repeatedly in His Word that He has a special tenderness for fatherless children and their mothers. There are many references in Scripture to their plight. For example:

- Deuteronomy 10:17-18: The Lord your God... defends the cause of the fatherless and the widow, and loves the alien, giving him food and clothing.
- Deuteronomy 27:19: Cursed is the man who withholds justice from the alien, the fatherless or the widow.
- Psalm 68:5: A father to the fatherless, a defender of widows is God in his holy dwelling.
- Zechariah 7:10: Do not oppress the widow or the fatherless, the alien or the poor.

... you as a single mother must make an all-out effort to find a father substitute for your boys.

Placing your boys under the influence of such a man for even a single hour per week can make a great difference.

...do not let the years go by without a man's influence in the lives of your boys. If they have no nurturing male role models by which to pattern themselves, they will turn to whoever is available, such as gang members, or perhaps, to you, the mom. And as we know, it is not healthy for boys to model themselves exclusively after their mothers.

... speaking ... to Christians who live in intact families. You have been reading in this chapter about the challenges faced by single parents. I hope you will consider the ways you might help. Men, how about taking the sons of single mothers with your own boys when you're going fishing or out to a ball game? Let those fatherless boys know that you care for them. Answer their questions and teach them how to throw a ball or how to block and tackle.[5]

Every Man's a Mentor, Sam Mehaffie, Forward by Dr. Ken Canfield

> I am convinced that our responsibilities as men and fathers extend far beyond our own families. A faithful father has no choice about attending to the matters of the Father. One of those matters is clearly coming to the aid of the fatherless, the orphan and the distressed. God is "a father to the fatherless, a defender of widows. He sets the lonely in families" (Psalm 68:5-6). If we fail in our mission to build a bridge to the fatherless, then our churches, communities, cities and nations as we know them will melt down.[6]

Consider this: If every young man who grew up in an intact family stayed committed to a life long marriage, but every young man who left home from a broken family struggled with the idea of marriage commitment, our nation would likely continue in a downward spiral of dysfunctional families. Only 34 percent of all children born in America will live with both biological parents through age eighteen.[7] And remember from chapter 4, with divorce rates at 50% or more, a study showed that three years after divorce, less than half the men ever see their kids again ... *ever!* Also, 36.8% of births last year were to unmarried women.[8] These fatherless kids must be given a model of God's plan for marriage. That often means a non-family mentor who is willing to step in and expand his influence. That means you and me.

OUR GENERATION OF MEN

As I said earlier in this chapter, men are resistant to change. They are set in their ways. Even when they agree with a need for change in their own lives, affecting that change is another matter. Some men, however, reach a breaking point that sends them over the edge, enough for them to finally transform out of their old ways. The catalyst for this change will vary, but I'm suggesting a prospect that I hope and pray will influence men to change. I'm referring, of course, to the future of our boys.

I pray that the information and ideas in the first four chapters of this book have had a huge impact on you. I hope you understand the effects of culture on our boys. I hope you also understand your power and influence on your family, especially your sons. I pray that you are so compelled to come through for your family, and specifically your sons, that you are now ready for change. Read on and see how your commitment to modeling and mentoring manhood will help make you into the man you want to be and the man God created you to be. Furthermore, we will conclude with the picture of the compounded return of your influence for generations to come.

What the Bible Says About … Being a Man, J. Richard Fugate

Most men in the 21st century have been raised mostly by female caregivers. In many cases fathers did not even know what to teach their sons about being a man. Indeed, most of *their* dads did not know.

…fathers will need to discover Biblical manhood for themselves and then teach their sons quality character traits by word and by deed. Until that happens, our country will continue accepting the consequences of our lack of proper masculine leadership.

Are you willing to commit yourself to stop abandoning your sons and to make the sacrifice necessary to train them to be men? Of course, this means that you will need to commit to learn and practice

Biblical manhood yourself. You and your son *could* learn and become mature together.[9]

Raising a Modern-Day Knight, Robert Lewis

If you are serious about your assignment, I suspect you'll make an effort, first of all, to clean out your own closet. You will take to heart the importance of your own character and lifestyle. The father who diligently improves his own character and spiritual life can jump-start his son… it is that important.[10]

OUR GENERATION OF WIVES AND CHILDREN

If you make changes to become the mentor your son needs, you also become the man your wife and daughters need. The new you that models and teaches Biblical manhood will carry out God's plan for you as a husband and father. The new you will lead and serve the family with Christ-likeness.

Bringing Up Boys, James Dobson

Men were designed to take care of the people they love, even if it involves personal sacrifice. When they fulfill that responsibility, their wives, sons, and daughters usually live in greater peace and harmony.[11]

Maximized Manhood, Ed Cole

Whenever a man changes and becomes the man God wants him to be, it will bring change to the woman and the children. … The whole home changes when the man changes.[12]

Point Man, Steve Farrar

To the wife it should be said that the form your submission takes will vary according to the quality of your husband's leadership. If the husband is a godly man who has a biblical vision for the family and leads out in the things of the Spirit, a godly wife will rejoice in this leadership and support him in it.[13]

I believe Scripture teaches that the husband is the head of the marriage relationship, and the wife is to ultimately submit to his authority. But I also believe that a man should not demand submission from his wife. Instead, he should be such an exemplary model of submission to the authorities in his own life that he provides the kind of leadership at home that is easy to follow.

[Mutual submission] does mean that the husband demonstrates and models the concept of submission in his own life when the situation calls for such a response.[14]

THE WIVES AND CHILDREN OF THE NEXT GENERATION

If the target group of mentoring our sons and the fatherless boys is tomorrow's men, and if changed men effect the whole home, then mentoring the men of tomorrow will affect the entirety of tomorrow's families. The wives and children of our boys will live in greater peace and harmony.

The Wonder of Boys, Michael Gurion

Every time you raise a loving, wise, and responsible man, you have created a better world for a woman. Women [today] are having to bond to half-men, with

139

boys who were not fully raised to manhood, don't know how to bond, and don't have a strong sense of service.[15]

Dad the Family Mentor, Dave Simmons

The true measure of fatherhood is not what you accomplish with your children but the extent of godliness in your grandchildren. In Deuteronomy 4:9, Moses wrote: ... but make them known to your sons and grandsons.[16]

Point Man, Steve Farrar

Little boys are the hope of the next generation. They are the fathers of tomorrow. They must know who they are and what they are to do.[17]

THE STATUS QUO

Today, however, we can identify a status quo among men. While there are always data points above and below the bell curve, the behavior of today's typical men can still be defined by certain parameters. It's clear that, over the years, these behaviors have strayed from God's plan. As we have previously made clear, these typical behaviors include over commitment to work and under commitment to family.

Unfortunately, maintaining a status quo actually results in a downward spiral. Because children typically follow the patterns set by their parents, and 66% of the kids today are leaving broken or dysfunctional homes by age eighteen,[18] the families of tomorrow are likely to exhibit more brokenness and dysfunction than today's.

At this point I'd like to borrow some stats reported by S. Truett Cathy, founder of Chick-fil-a. In his book *It's Better to Build Boys Than Mend Men*, he shares this:

The Results of Fatherlessness

The United States is the world's leader in father-less homes. The results of our actions, according to the Fathers' Manifesto:

63% of youth suicides are from fatherless homes.
90% of all homeless and runaway children are from fatherless homes.
80% of rapists motivated with displaced angers come from fatherless homes.
71% of all high school dropouts come from father-less homes.
85% of youth in prisons grew up in fatherless homes.
75% of all adolescent patients in drug treatment centers come from fatherless homes.

Children From Fatherless Homes Are:

5 times more likely to commit suicide
32 times more likely to run away
20 times more likely to have behavioral disorders
14 times more likely to commit rape
9 times more likely to drop out of school
10 times more likely to abuse chemical substances
9 times more likely to end up in a state-operated institution
20 times more likely to end up in prison[19]

Oh, but there's more. Among the children suffering from fatherlessness, boys are feeling the brunt of the effects. I offered a portion of this in Chapter 2, but pay attention to this. From Dobson's *Bringing Up Boys*:

> Boys, when compared to girls, are six times more likely to have learning disabilities, three times more likely to be registered drug addicts, and four times more likely to be diagnosed as emotionally disturbed. They are at greater risk for schizophrenia, autism, sexual addiction, alcoholism, bed wetting, and all forms of antisocial and criminal behavior. They are twelve times more likely to murder someone, and their rate of death in car accidents is greater by 50 percent. Seventy-seven percent of delinquency-related court cases involve males. There is more. Boys younger than fifteen years of age are twice as likely to be admitted to psychiatric hospitals and five times more likely than girls to kill themselves. Fully 80 percent of suicides involves males under twenty-five years of age. Suicide among black adolescent boys has increased 165 percent just in the past twelve years. Boys comprise 90 percent of those in drug treatment programs and 95 percent of kids involved in juvenile court.[20]

Conclusion: Fatherlessness breads fatherlessness. And these numbers account only for homes with *physically* absent fathers. They are compounded by the effects of mentally absent or abusive fathers. And we see just another example of the rule of compound return – in the wrong direction.

So what's to be done? One single mom contacted Big Brothers. They're in the business of providing just what she and her son needed – a male role model. Their answer: "We have more requests for male mentors but have more female volunteers. Can we give you a 'big sister' for your son?" I think they missed the point.

Just a guess, but I would venture to say we probably have more than ten boys in need of a mentor for every adult male volunteer, maybe a hundred. We've got to find another way. We've got to reach the boys where they are. We've got to mentor within the existing male youth programs. We've got to bring back Christ-centered manhood by teaching it to *all young men.*

ALL GENERATIONS TO FOLLOW

Can we affect that much change through mentorship of our teen boys? I believe we can. The next generation of men, including the fatherless, our generation of men, our wives and children, and the wives and children of the next generation – all will benefit. But the benefit doesn't stop there.

Season of Life, Jeffrey Marx, quoting Joe Ehrmann

"All these problems I've been trying to deal with [poverty, racism, drugs, crime, illiteracy, family disintegration], they're not just problems, they're also symptoms, ... They're symptoms of the single biggest failure of our society. We simply don't do a good enough job of teaching boys how to be men."[21]

Family Man – Family Leader, Philip Lancaster

Our national crisis is a consequence of the crisis of the home, and the crisis of the home is a crisis of male leadership.[22]

Seven Promises of a Promise Keeper

May I remind you of one historical fact: No nation has ever survived the disintegration of its home life.

Once the home goes, it's just a question of time before it all goes.[23]

Point Man, Steve Farrar

"If I could offer a single prescription for the survival of America, and particularly black America," wrote William Raspberry, a black columnist with the *Washington Post*, "it would be to restore the family. And if you asked me how to do it, my answer – doubtlessly oversimplified – would be: save the boys."

If our boys are not equipped to lead families, then the families of the next generation will not have leaders. And neither will the next, for it becomes a vicious epidemic that multiplies with each successive generation.[24]

It is the responsibility of the parents, and ultimately that of the father, to make sure the children grow up in an environment that will enable them to one day become competent, responsible parents in their own right. This ensures the continuity of the biblical family for the next generation.

It is abundantly clear that one of the goals of the enemy is to interrupt this link of biblical families from generation to generation. He does this by implementing two strategies:

Strategy #1: *To effectively alienate and sever a husband's relationship with his wife.* Such a division can either be physical or emotional. Both are equally effective.

Strategy #2: *To effectively alienate and sever a father's relationship with his children.* Again, such division can either be physical or emotional. Both are equally effective.[25]

And if there are no masculine men and feminine women for the next generation or the ones to follow, then you might as well go ahead and shut this country down.[26]

Bringing Up Boys, James Dobson

...I believe the future of Western civilization depends on how we handle this present crisis. Why? Because we as parents are raising the next generation of men who will either lead with honor and integrity or abandon every good thing they have inherited. They are the bridges to the future. Nations that are populated largely by immature, immoral, weak-willed, cowardly, and self-indulgent men cannot and will not long endure. These types of men include those who sire and abandon their children; who cheat on their wives; who lie, steal, and covet; who hate their countrymen; and who serve no god but money. That is the direction culture is taking today's boys. We must make the necessary investment to counter these influences and to build within our boys lasting qualities of character, self-discipline, respect for authority, commitment to the truth, a belief in the work ethic, and an unshakable love for Jesus Christ.[27]

Psalm 33:11 (*italics mine*)

But the plans of the LORD stand firm forever,
the purpose of his heart through *all generations.*

The hope of our nation's future rides on the families of tomorrow. The hope of the families rides on the men of tomorrow. The hope of the men of tomorrow rides on the boys of today. The hope is in our hands as we follow Christ and His plan – then share Him and His plan with our boys.

12 Teaching Topics For Christ-Centered Manhood

I have derived twelve teaching topics from the following three scriptures. I call them Knighthood Verses. The teaching topics from the verses will provide you with a well-defined set of ideals and a biblically grounded definition of manhood.

The resources offered by Squires2Knights Ministries will draw from these twelve teaching topics. In order to catalog the devotions and lessons, the twelve topics have been numbered according to the applicable verse: 1, 2, and 3; then by the character trait within the verse; i.e. 1.1, 2.4, 3.2.

1. And Jesus grew in wisdom, stature, and in favor with God and men (Luke 2:52).

"And Jesus grew..." Jesus was twelve years old when his parents found him in the temple courts of Jerusalem with the teachers. His teen-age years of growing and maturing followed.

1.1: Wisdom: From a biblical worldview, we use of our knowledge, discernment, and understanding to take the right course of action.

1.2: Stature: Physical nourishment, growth, strength and health.

1.3: Favor with God: Follow God's will through faith, discipleship, prayer, love and service.

1.4: Favor with men: Socially competent. Able to gain the respect of people and to influence others.

2. Be on your guard, stand firm in the faith, *act like men (be men of courage)*; be strong. Do everything in love (1 Corinthians 16:13, 14).

2.1: Be on your guard: A call to fight against temptations from Satan, from the world, and from our selves. It also helps guide us toward self-control. Finally, we are called to be alert, always prepared for Jesus' return.

2.2: Stand firm in the faith: The center of what gives meaning and purpose to our lives through Jesus Christ. Ultimately, it is our faith in Christ as our Lord that assures our salvation and it is our identity in Christ that directs our heart, mind and soul to the nature and character of God.

2.3: Act like men (be men of courage): This is the central theme for our lessons and discussions. This proclamation implores us to pursue our divine roles as men. Biblically, we are to be disciples, servants, husbands, fathers and finally, patriarchs. Not all men will be called to fulfill every one of these roles. Some of these roles will be carried out during different seasons of life. To fulfill these roles, we are called to spiritual leadership and servant leadership. We are to be the provider and protector. In this directive from Paul, the original text refers to a masculine *courage*.

2.4: Be strong: Strong in faith, strong in character, strong in perseverance, strong in body. This statement dovetails with our roles as leader, provider and protector.

2.5: Do: Implies being proactive, not passive or reactive. "Released from the law...we serve in newness of the Spirit," proving ourselves "doers of the word." As the Lord's Prayer says: "Thy will be done."

2.6: Everything in love: Sums up the law (Galatians 5:14) and implies a selfless, servant attitude.

3. And just as we have borne the likeness of the earthly man, so shall we bear the likeness of the man from heaven (1 Corinthians 15:49).

3.1: Adam, the earthly man: We are born as the first Adam (Hebrew for man): self-centered, worldly in our flesh and full of sin.

3.2: Christ, the man from heaven: Our "righteousness from God comes through faith in Jesus Christ" and we have "put on a new self" through Christ. No longer "under the law" of the old covenant, our identity "in Christ" directs our heart, mind, and soul to the nature and character of Jesus Christ, the "life-giving spirit." Christ-likeness.

Endnotes

Forward

1. *Family Man, Family Leader*, Philip Lancaster, (The Vision Forum, Inc., 2003), 16

Chapter 1, Who Gives the Rite of Passage?

1. *Men of Iron*, Howard Pyle, (Harper & Brothers Publishers, 1891), revised from pages 222-228
2. Steve Farrar, *Point Man*, (Multnomah Publishers, Inc., 2003), 210
3. Steve Farrar, *Point Man*, (Multnomah Publishers, Inc., 2003), 207, 210
4. John Eldredge, *Wild at Heart*, (Thomas Nelson Publishers, 2001), 62
5. John Eldredge, *Wild at Heart*, (Thomas Nelson Publishers, 2001), 71-72
6. John Eldredge, *The Way of the Wild Heart*, (Thomas Nelson, Inc., 2006), 6
7. Robert Lewis, *Raising a Modern-Day Knight*, (Tyndale House Publishers, 1997), 10
8. Robert Lewis, *Raising a Modern-Day Knight*, (Tyndale House Publishers, 1997), 103
9. Robert Lewis, *Raising a Modern-Day Knight*, (Tyndale House Publishers, 1997), 99

Chapter 2, Dad vs. Culture

1. *Star Wars Episode II, Attack of the Clones*, Lucas Film Ltd., 2002
2. *Star Wars Episode II, Attack of the Clones*, Lucas Film Ltd., 2002
3. *Star Wars Episode II, Attack of the Clones*, Lucas Film Ltd., 2002
4. Blaine Bartel, *Let Me Tell You What Your Teens Are Telling Me*, (Harrison House Press, 2005)
5. Blaine Bartel, *Let Me Tell You What Your Teens Are Telling Me*, (Harrison House Press, 2005)
6. James Dobson, *Bringing Up Boys*, (Tyndale House Publishers, 2001), 89-90
7. Robert Lewis, *Raising a Modern-Day Knight*, (Tyndale House Publishers, 1997), 157
8. Robert Lewis, *Raising a Modern-Day Knight*, (Tyndale House Publishers, 1997), 66
9. S. Truett Cathy, *It's Better to Build Boys Than Mend Men*, (Looking Glass Books, 2004), in the Forward by Art Linkletter, 7
10. Wendy Kock, "Groups aim to 'plant seeds' with kids," *USA Today, November 22, 2006, 6A*
11. James Dobson, *Bringing Up Boys*, (Tyndale House Publishers, 2001), 102-103
12. James Dobson, *Bringing Up Boys*, (Tyndale House Publishers, 2001), 107
13. David Barton, *Original Intent*, (Wallbuilder Press, 1999), 24-36
14. Neda Ulably, "MTV at 25: From Upstart to Parent Network," www.npr.org, August 1, 2006
15. "Bringing Up Boys Videos," *Focus on the Family, November 2002*, 3
16. S. Truett Cathy, *It's Better to Build Boys Than Mend Men*, (Looking Glass Books, 2004), 67

17. Kevin Leman, *Adolescence Isn't Terminal*, (Tyndale House Publishers, 2002), 53
18. Dave Simmons, *Dad the Family Mentor*, (Victor Books, 1992), 17
19. James Dobson, *Bringing Up Boys*, (Tyndale House Publishers, 2001), 33
20. "Bringing Up Boys Videos," *Focus on the Family, November 2002*, 3
21. Josh McDowell, *PK2000, Go the Distance*, Dallas, TX, (CTI Conference Services, 2000), Session 4
22. James Dobson, *Bringing Up Boys*, (Tyndale House Publishers, 2001), 223-224
23. Kevin Leman, *Adolescence Isn't Terminal*, (Tyndale House Publishers, 2002), 80, 114
24. Joe White, *Sticking With Your Teen*, (Tyndale House Publishers, 2006), 9-10
25. Dave Simmons, *Dad the Family Mentor*, (Victor Books, 1992), 54

Chapter 3, From Role Model to Mentor

1. James Dobson, *Bringing Up Boys*, (Tyndale House Publishers, 2001), 181
2. James Dobson, *Bringing Up Boys*, (Tyndale House Publishers, 2001), 181
3. John Eldredge, *Wild at Heart*, (Thomas Nelson Publishers, 2001), 80-81
4. J. Richard Fugate, *What The Bible Says About...Being A Man*, (Foundation for Bible Research, 2002), 42
5. Hannah Cleaverin Berlin, "Lads Night Out Can Save Your Marriage," *London Daily Express*, 25 April 2000
6. James Dobson, *Bringing Up Boys*, (Tyndale House Publishers, 2001), 58
7. James Dobson, *Bringing Up Boys*, (Tyndale House Publishers, 2001), 90

8. John Eldredge, *Wild at Heart*, (Thomas Nelson Publishers, 2001), 62
9. Gary Smalley and John Trent, Ph.D., *The Hidden Value of a Man*, (Focus on the Family Publishing, 1992), 119
10. James Dobson, *Bringing Up Boys*, (Tyndale House Publishers, 2001), 120
11. Brian Molitor, *Boy's Passage – Man's Journey*, (Emerald Books, 2004), 22
12. Merriam Webster Online, 2006, http://mw1.merriam-webster.com/dictionary/role%20model
13. *American Dictionary of the English Language, Noah Webster 1828, Facsimile First Addition*, (Foundation for American Christian Education, 1995), "model"
14. Dave Simmons, *Dad the Family Mentor*, (Victor Books, 1992), 51-52
15. Douglas Southall Freeman, *R.E. Lee* vol. I (New York: Macmillan, 1934), 178
16. Robert Lewis, *Raising a Modern-Day Knight*, (Tyndale House Publishers, 1997), 24
17. James Dobson, *Bringing Up Boys*, (Tyndale House Publishers, 2001), 75-77
18. Sam Mehaffie, *Every Man's a Mentor*, (Xulon Press, 2005), xix
19. Brian Molitor, *Boy's Passage – Man's Journey*, (Emerald Books, 2004), 135
20. Robert Lewis, *Raising a Modern-Day Knight*, (Tyndale House Publishers, 1997), 15
21. *Seven Promises of a Promise Keeper*, (Focus on the Family Publishing, 1994), 45
22. Dennis Rainy, Family Life Ministries, "Manhood", taped presentation at a business conference.
23. Phillips, Craig and Dean, *Lifeline*, "I Want to Be Just Like You," (Star Song, 1994)

Chapter 4, Mentoring Priorities

1. Harry Chapin, *Verities & Balderdash*, "Cats in the Cradle," (Electra Records, 1974)
2. James Dobson, *Bringing Up Boys*, (Tyndale House Publishers, 2001), 106
3. Rita Rubin, "Birthrate among teenagers drops to record low," *USA Today*, November 22, 2006, 6A
4. Dave Simmons, *Dad the Family Mentor*, (Victor Books, 1992), 50
5. Dave Simmons, *Dad the Family Mentor*, (Victor Books, 1992), 33
6. Robert Lewis, "Raising a Modern-Day Knight," (Tyndale House Publishers, 1997), 83
7. Dave Simmons, *Dad the Family Mentor*, (Victor Books, 1992), Forward by Howard G. Hendricks, 11-12
8. Robert Lewis, "Raising a Modern-Day Knight," (Tyndale House Publishers, 1997), 83
9. Edwin Louis Cole, *Sexual Integrity*, (Watercolor books,1992, 1997), 96-98
10. Sam Mehaffie, *Every Man's a Mentor*, (Xulon Press, 2005), 25
11. Steve Farrar, *Point Man*, (Multnomah Publishers, Inc., 2003), 30

Chapter 5, Squires

1. Robert Lewis, *Raising a Modern-Day Knight*, (Tyndale House Publishers, 1997), 150-151
2. Gary Smalley and John Trent, Ph.D., *The Hidden Value of a Man*, (Focus on the Family Publishing, 1992), 135-138
3. Jeffrey Marx, *Season of Life*, (Simon and Schuster, 2003), 28-29
4. Sam Mehaffie, *Every Man's a Mentor*, (Xulon Press, 2005), 54

5. Steve Chapman, *10 Things I Want My Son to Know*, (Harvest House Publishers, 2002), 108
6. Jeremy V. Jones, *Focus on the Family, October 2005*, 12
7. *The Boy Scout Handbook, Eleventh Edition*, (Boy Scouts of America, 1998)
8. *Seven Promises of a Promise Keeper*, (Focus on the Family Publishing, 1994)
9. Robert Lewis, *Raising a Modern-Day Knight*, (Tyndale House Publishers, 1997)
10. J. Richard Fugate, *What The Bible Says About...Being A Man*, (Foundation for Bible Research, 2002), 42
11. Dennis Rainey, *Steps to Manhood*, audiocassette tape, (Family Life, 2002)
12. James Dobson, *Bringing Up Boys*, (Tyndale House Publishers, 2001), 106
13. Sam Mehaffie, *Every Man's a Mentor*, (Xulon Press, 2005), 45
14. Josh McDowell, *The Father Connection*, (Broadman & Holman Publishers, 1996), 161
15. John Eldredge, *The Way of the Wild Heart*, (Thomas Nelson, Inc., 2006), 6

Chapter 9, Guy Kinda Fun
1. Andrew Sullivan, "The He Hormone," *New York Times Magazine*, 2 April 2000, 46
2. James Dobson, *Bringing Up Boys*, (Tyndale House Publishers, 2001), 25
3. John Eldredge, *Wild at Heart*, (Thomas Nelson Publishers, 2001), 13
4. John Eldredge, *Wild at Heart*, (Thomas Nelson Publishers, 2001), 35

Chapter 10, Rule of Compounded Return

1. Robert Lewis, *Raising a Modern-Day Knight*, (Tyndale House Publishers, 1997), 55
2. Dave Simmons, *Dad the Family Mentor*, (Victor Books, 1992), 50
3. Dennis Rainey, *Steps to Manhood*, audiocassette tape, (Family Life, 2002)
4. Harold Davis, *TALKS Mentoring of Champaign County*, Illinois
5. James Dobson, *Bringing Up Boys*, (Tyndale House Publishers, 2001), 137-143
6. Sam Mehaffie, *Every Man's a Mentor*, (Xulon Press, 2005), Forward by Dr. Ken Canfield, xi
7. Bureau of the Census, *Code Blue* (Washington, D.C.)
8. Rita Rubin, "Birthrate among teenagers drops to record low," *USA Today*, November 22, 2006, 6A
9. J. Richard Fugate, *What The Bible Says About...Being A Man*, (Foundation for Bible Research, 2002), 42
10. Robert Lewis, *Raising a Modern-Day Knight*, (Tyndale House Publishers, 1997), 148
11. James Dobson, *Bringing Up Boys*, (Tyndale House Publishers, 2001), 72
12. Edwin Louis Cole, *Maximized Manhood*, (Whitaker House, 1982), 105
13. Steve Farrar, *Point Man*, (Multnomah Publishers, Inc., 2003), 152
14. Steve Farrar, *Point Man*, (Multnomah Publishers, Inc., 2003), 165-166
15. Michael Gurion, *The Wonder of Boys*, (New York: Jeremy Tarcher/Putnam, 1996)
16. Dave Simmons, *Dad the Family Mentor*, (Victor Books, 1992), 19
17. Steve Farrar, *Point Man*, (Multnomah Publishers, Inc., 2003), 44
18. Bureau of the Census, *Code Blue* (Washington, D.C.)

19. S. Truett Cathy, *It's Better to Build Boys Than Mend Men*, (Looking Glass Books, 2004), 14
20. James Dobson, *Bringing Up Boys*, (Tyndale House Publishers, 2001), 33
21. Jeffrey Marx, *Season of Life*, (Simon and Schuster, 2003), 28
22. *Family Man, Family Leader*, Philip Lancaster, (The Vision Forum, Inc., 2003), 16
23. *Seven Promises of a Promise Keeper*, (Focus on the Family Publishing, 1994), 49
24. Steve Farrar, *Point Man*, (Multnomah Publishers, Inc., 2003), 36, 38
25. Steve Farrar, *Point Man*, (Multnomah Publishers, Inc., 2003), 25-26
26. Steve Farrar, *Point Man*, (Multnomah Publishers, Inc., 2003), 170-171
27. James Dobson, *Bringing Up Boys*, (Tyndale House Publishers, 2001), 54

Printed in the United States
200929BV00002B/1-156/A